Series editor's foreword

Derek Rowntree has a unique talent. He is able to distil years of experience into highly readable texts to leave the reader stimulated and with a host of questions to answer and issues to explore. In this book, *Making Materials-Based Learning Work*, Derek succeeds in his two key tasks. First, he introduces a new term to the field, 'materials-based learning' (MBL), and argues eloquently for its adoption. He reveals the limitations of several existing terms (including open and distance learning!) and clearly portrays the challenging role available to you as a teacher or trainer wanting the best for your learners. Second, he offers a superb set of briefing notes that spans three key areas:

- setting up and managing an MBL programme or system;
- setting up a learner support system;
- designing courses and learning materials.

These inform and challenge both the novice and experienced producer alike. His entries range from 'Access' to 'Developmental testing', 'Market research' to 'Workload', 'Cheating' to 'Readability', with the opportunity for numerous cross-links. Derek shares his experience and insights yet always gives you the opportunity to interpret the questions he poses in relation to your own situation; to make the learning yours.

While his subtitle, 'Principles, politics and practicalities', does reinforce the focus of the book, an alternative subtitle might have been 'All you wanted to know but were afraid to ask'. Those who are already familiar with Derek's books will not be disappointed by this one. Even at the very end of the book he demonstrates his commitment to materials-based learning by providing an annotated list of further reading and useful Internet sources.

I am sure your study of the entries in this book, and further consideration of the questions the author poses, will repay your investment and benefit your colleagues and your learners. Using one of his own terms, I believe Derek will recruit a whole army of 'champions'.

Fred Lockwood

photo by Mike Levers

Before we begin . . .

In case you've not seen previous books of mine, here are one or two things you
may find helpful to know about where your author is 'coming from'. I have been
working with materials-based learning for more than 35 years. First with
'programmed learning', next with 'independent learning' and 'resource-based
learning', then, since 1970, with open/distance learning in the Open University
and, most recently, with 'flexible learning', with 'resource-based learning' making
a come-back and with the newly arrived technology-based teaching.

Over the years I've worked in a variety of subject areas, including humanities,
education, health care and management education. In recent years – partly
through my consultancies and workshops for outside organisations – I have
mostly been concerned with materials-based approaches to vocational training
and professional updating. I have, for example, helped develop the use of open
and distance learning in police training and management education.

As well as learning materials, I have written several books for course developers
– like *Teaching through Self-instruction*, *Exploring Open and Distance Learning*,
Preparing Materials for Open, Distance and Flexible Learning and *Teaching with Audio
in Open and Flexible Learning*.

Despite (or maybe because of) all this experience, I am still not sanguine about the
future of materials-based learning. It's not as easy as it sometimes looks – not in
any of its many forms. Over the years, I've seen them come and I've seen them go.
I have written this book as my contribution to ensuring that materials-based
learning survives and evolves for as long as it can be of use.

Derek Rowntree, 1997

Making Materials-Based Learning Work

Principles, politics and practicalities

DEREK ROWNTREE

**KOGAN
PAGE**

London • Stirling (USA)

Open and Distance Learning Series

Series Editor: Fred Lockwood

Activities in Self-Instructional Texts, Fred Lockwood
Becoming an Effective Open and Distance Learner, Perc Marland
Exploring Open and Distance Learning, Derek Rowntree
Improving Your Students' Learning, Alistair Morgan
Key Terms and Issues in Open and Distance Learning, Barbara Hodgson
Managing Open Systems, Richard Freeman
Mega-Universities and Knowledge Media, John S Daniel
Objectives, Competencies and Learning Outcomes, Reginald F Melton
Open and Distance Learning: Case Studies from Education, Industry and Commerce,
   Stephen Brown
Open and Flexible Learning in Vocational Education and Training, Judith Calder and Ann
   McCollum
Preparing Materials for Open, Distance and Flexible Learning, Derek Rowntree
Programme Evaluation and Quality, Judith Calder
Teaching Through Projects, Jane Henry
Teaching with Audio in Open and Distance Learning, Derek Rowntree
The Costs and Economics of Open and Distance Learning, Greville Rumble
Understanding Learners in Open and Distance Education, Terry Evans
Using Communications Media in Open and Flexbile Learning, Robin Mason

First published in 1997

Kogan Page Limited
120 Pentonville Road
London N1 9JN
and
22883 Quicksilver Drive
Stirling, VA 20166, USA

British Library Cataloguing in Publication Data

A CIP record for this book is available from the British Library.

ISBN 0 7494 2240 8

Typeset by the author
Printed and bound in Great Britain by Biddles Ltd, Guildford and King's Lynn

What's the problem?

I'd better begin by explaining this book's title. Like me, you probably think there's already more than enough jargon around in education and training . So why invent yet another term – 'materials-based learning'? Aren't there plenty of similar terms to choose from? Couldn't I have used any one of, for example:

- open learning
- distance learning
- flexible learning
- independent learning
- supported self-study
- self-managed learning
- computer-assisted learning
- technology-based teaching
- distributed teaching
- resource-based learning?

I considered doing so, but decided I couldn't. What I am talking about in this book is *all* of these forms of learning. I could hardly have included all these 'brand names' in my title. But there isn't a single term among them that includes all the others. These types of learning system all have their differences.

Fortunately, they do also have one central factor in common. In each case, learners depend far more on *materials*, and far less on face-to-face teaching, than they do in other types of learning system. That indeed is what this book is about – or, to be more precise, about how to design a materials-based learning system and keep it working effectively.

Materials-based learning systems are even more diverse than the terms used to label them. They are common in both education and training. Learners may be working at a centre (eg on campus or in their workplace) or in their homes. They may be spending just a few hours on a collection of learning materials or several years on a materials-based course. They may be meeting regularly with other learners and a tutor, or they may never set eyes on them. Their learning programme may include a substantial element of face-to-face contact; but it may include none at all. And they may or may not be doing other kinds of learning alongside, or in between, their materials-based activities.

Does this sound like I may be talking about the kind of learning system you are interested in? You've probably got a pretty fair idea by now. But you may be wondering: 'How much use of materials needs to be involved before we would say the system is materials-*based*?' After all, most learning systems involve some sort of materials, even if it's only textbooks or lecture notes.

In the diagram below, I'm suggesting a continuum between face-to-face learning and materials-based learning. As we move from left to right, more and more of the learner's time is spent with materials and less and less in face-to-face contact with a teacher or trainer. At what point we choose to say the system becomes materials-based is debatable – eg 25 per cent of the learner's time on materials, 50 per cent, 75 per cent?

But does it matter?

I would suggest that *any* shift from whatever is your present position towards greater dependence on materials (and less on face-to-face contact) may open up many new learning opportunities – while at the same time presenting a number of new challenges and potential problems.

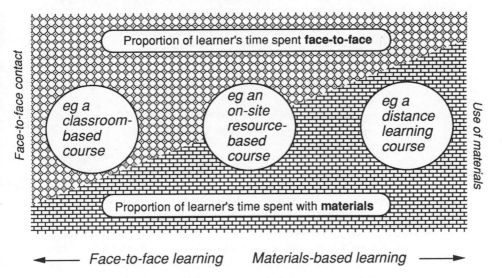

Why this book?

I've written this book because setting up and running a materials-based learning system is not as easy as it looks. This is what people who come on my workshops, from both the educational and the training world, keep telling me. I get asked questions like:

- 'Why can't we convince our bosses?'
- 'Why are the tutors/trainers so suspicious?'
- 'Why don't other people co-operate?'
- 'Why are our learners reluctant to start and prone to give up too soon?'
- 'Why did it get to be so expensive?'
- 'Why isn't it working?'

What most of them soon realize is that materials alone are not enough. Even the most exquisitely formed workbooks, videos, audio-tapes, computer programs and multimedia extravaganzas may turn out to be useless. If your learners don't get to hear about them, or get them at the wrong time, or are not properly introduced to them, or are given no encouragement and have no one to talk to if they run into difficulties, and are not assessed on what they might have learned – then we need hardly be surprised if they don't learn very much.

It is not enough to pour money into buying glossy learning packages or providing rooms full of computers. Unless we plan and implement effective systems for development, delivery and learner support, such expense will mostly be wasted. This book is about the principles, politics and practicalities of doing so. How can we make materials-based learning work?

What can you do?

What you can do will depend on who you are. More precisely, it will depend on which aspects of open learning you are concerned with and what your role is. For example:

- If you are a developer of learning materials, you may want to argue for certain kinds of support being made available to learners while they are using those materials.

- If you are a tutor or a trainer whose job it is to support the learners, you may be wondering what you are expected to provide that the materials cannot.

- If you are the manager of an open learning system, you may have a variety of concerns – from negotiating goals and resources with your bosses or clients to winning the effective co-operation of a range of full-time and part-time staff.

Whatever your role and area of concern, you'll probably find it necessary to pay attention to other people's concerns as well as your own. Materials-based learning systems are more dependent than most on the combined efforts of a variety of specialists. Your ability to get satisfactory results yourself may thus depend on what other people are doing (or not doing).

Will people in education face the same opportunities and challenges as people in training? No, of course not. In fact, I thought of offering two versions of this book – one for teachers and one for trainers. But I decided against it. Although each group has concerns of its own, they also have much in common. Indeed, the differences among teachers and among trainers are probably greater than the differences between the two groups. And, more to the point, there are few concerns of one group that will not resonate with certain concerns of the other group. We are all in this together.

What might you get from this book?

This book offers a variety of ways of making materials-based learning work. You won't be able to apply all of them yourself. But you may want to press for other people to apply them. And you may have some of them applied to you!

There is no sure-fire recipe for success in materials-based learning. So I can't suggest a step-by-step procedure that will get you from where you are to where you want to be. I'm sure you are too worldly-wise to expect it. So what will you be getting in this book?

What I've done is pick out a number of concepts or issues that seem to give us a handle on improving things. We can think of these as potential 'success factors'. (Or, of course, if not dealt with in a way appropriate to your situation, as potential failure factors.) I've written a briefing note (no more than one page) about each factor, in the hope of stimulating your own thinking. Of course, I can't say everything about anything in just one page. But I hope I've said enough to help you decide whether the factor is relevant to your situation and, if so, what are some of the key aspects and whether there are any potential difficulties you'll need to look out for.

No doubt I could have woven these factors into some kind of continuous argument that would split conventionally into chapters and sections. But I believe that the factors will have more impact if you come across them in random order.

So I've done my best to avoid a linear presentation. Ideally, I might have presented you with a box of shufflable cards which you could read in any order you chose. I've done the next best thing by arranging the factors in A–Z order. Start where you like and go on to wherever you please.

You will, however, find plenty of cross-references between one factor and another. Few of them can be considered in isolation from at least some of the others.

To use the current multimedia jargon, this book takes a 'hypertext' approach. Words I have printed in **bold** type are like buttons in multimedia that you can 'press' to get into a fuller discussions of that concept. Look up any word or phrase I've thus indicated and you should find another relevant pageful. No doubt you'll keep coming up against the same factor in a number of different contexts. I make no apology for this. Repetition (with variations) is a time-honoured teaching technique. The variety of contexts should help you develop your own, personal 'take' on each factor.

However, you may not wish to dip in at random or work through the book from A to Z. So, on page 6, you will see I have indicated which factors are likely to be of primary interest to people in each of the three main roles mentioned above. However, the way I have portioned them out is quite rough and ready. Most factors will have some relevance for people in any of the three roles. And many will be relevant to people with yet other roles, eg librarians, learning centre receptionists and learners' line managers.

The Further Reading section at the end of the book should give you plenty of help with finding out more about our factors (and others). In case you are an Internet user, I have mentioned there and elsewhere a few relevant World Wide Web sites that I have visited lately. I can't, of course, guarantee that they will still be available when you come to read this book. But no doubt new ones will still be setting up every day.

Inevitably, of course, you and other readers may want to ask 'Why has he devoted a page to factors P, Q or R when he's given no space at all to factors X, Y and Z?' All I can say is that I've chosen what I see as the key factors at present. If you believe others are more deserving of space, let me know and I'll perhaps be able to work them into the next edition.

Best wishes for the success of your own ventures into MBL. If you feel like telling me about them, my e-mail address is:

d.g.f.rowntree@open.ac.uk

Making materials-based learning work

A few of the factors you may need to think about

Setting up and managing an MBL programme or system

Access
Accountancy
Accreditation
Aims
Alumni
Anticipation
APL
Appraisal
Attitudes
Benefits
Briefing
Case studies
Champions
Cheating
Collaboration
Communication
Competition
Consultants
Consultation
Contracts
Costing MBL
Course
    specification
Credibility
Customers
Debriefing
Definitions
Distance
Economics
Failure
Feelings
Institutional
    support
Job descriptions
Learning systems
Managing MBL
Market research
Monitoring
Needs analysis
Networking
Newsletters
Ownership
Production
Quality assurance
Record-keeping
Resistance
Rewards
Roles
Scheduling
Staff development
Stress
Teams
Trojan horses
Workshops

Setting up a learner support system

Centres
Conferencing
Correspondence
    teaching
Drop-outs
Effectiveness
Entry counselling
Evaluation
Face-to-face
    sessions
Feedback
Glue
Help lines
Individualization
Lectures
Libraries
Line managers
Mentors
Milieu
Self-help groups
Study skills
Support
Tutors

Designing courses and learning materials

Activities
Assessment
Assignments
Commenting
Competition
Computerized
    testing
Content
Copyright
Course guides
Deadlines
Developmental
    testing
Diversity
Economies
Examinations
Existing materials
Flexibilities
Gradualism
Images of
    learning
Images of
    teaching
Integration
Interactivity
Internet
Learners
Learning styles
Materials
Media
Motivations
Objectives
Pacing
Packages
Practical work
Prerequisites
Projects
Readability
Structure
Study guides
Technology
Time
User-friendliness
Workload

Access—*getting into MBL*

For many teachers and trainers, improving access is one of their key **aims** in promoting materials-based learning. Followers of *open* learning, in particular, say they are trying to lower some of the many barriers that often stop people from learning. They could be talking about the barriers that deter people from enrolling for your programme in the first place. For instance, you may be:

- expecting too much by way of **prerequisites**

- charging too high a fee

- requiring **learners** attend at an inconvenient place or time

- basing the programme on **media** the learners cannot use

- offering it at an inconvenient time of year or day

- making it sound less congenial than it actually is.

Easing any one of these constraints might bring more learners into your programme. This is attractive to many teachers and trainers because easier access means more learners, and more learners mean more money – and even perhaps hanging on to one's job.

But what kind of 'more learners'? No problem, perhaps, if we are looking for more learners of the kind we have already. But we may be aiming to enrol 'less qualified' learners – perhaps even people who have not previously thought of themselves as learners – people who have been turned off or dumped by their earlier experience of schooling. In cases such as these, we may need to do rather more than revamp our marketing strategy and offer fee reductions.

After all, the open learning enthusiasts I mentioned in the opening paragraph above may not just be talking about lowering barriers that prevent people getting in. They may also be talking about barriers that prevent learners from doing well on the programme *after* they have got in. That is to say, we may need to improve not just access *to* the programme but also the accessibility (**user-friendliness**) *of* the programme. This can be costly.

'Improving access' is a cause that may sound beyond challenge (like 'motherhood' used to do). But, if you and your colleagues pursue it, you need to remember that it brings its own problems, contradictions and costs. In the end, one has to decide: how much more access, of what kind, and for whom?

Accountancy—*of the creative variety*

MBL adds up differently from 'traditional' learning. With traditional learning, there is very little up-front money needed for **materials**. Most of the costs come in salaries for staff once the course is under way. With MBL it is often the other way round: huge investments in staff time, consumables and equipment are often needed to develop and produce materials before any **learners** have even been recruited. Once the course is up and running, staff costs may be relatively light (compared with the numbers of learners involved). Yet the course budget may still need to make provision for the salary costs of **staff development**, of course **evaluation** and of updating, adding to and, eventually, rewriting the course materials.

So, if MBL is new to your organization, you might do well to ensure that your accountants understand just how it operates and what kinds of costs (and income) are involved at various points in the life history of a course. They may then be able to suggest many ways in which the funds can be massaged to flow to your best advantage.

If you win the sympathy of a creative accountant, he or she may, for example, be able to help you:

- set up a standard system for **costing MBL** projects
- spread the capital costs of equipment or developing materials over several years rather than just the first year
- get contributions from other budget-holders on account of **benefits** your MBL programme is bringing elsewhere in the organization – eg through increased output, learners losing less time away from work or fewer complaints
- predict potential income from selling copies of your own materials to other organizations and set it off against the cost of the programme
- save on development costs by working in **collaboration** with other organizations
- assess possible **economies** in course development
- find sponsors who will partly underwrite development costs or subsidize learners' fees
- resist the pressures from non-creative accountants (eg 'We could halve our paper bill by cutting out all this white space from your pages!') that might make you 'spoil the ship for a happorth of tar'.

Accountants can be strikingly imaginative, if we take the trouble to get them interested!

Accreditation—*credit wherever it's due*

A police officer recently told me that his attendance at several workshops of mine had been counted as credit towards an MA he'd done with his local university. This led me to wonder whether I should start advertising such possibilities as an added attraction to other potential attendees!

Getting 'a piece of paper to show for it' can be a useful source of **motivation** for **learners**. They know that the accreditation will be widely accepted as proof of their attainment.

Colleagues in education will not need reminding of this. There must be few courses in further and higher education that do not award some sort of certificate, diploma or degree. Alternatively, or sometimes in addition, such courses in the UK may also prepare candidates for National (or Scottish) Vocational Qualifications.

MBL programmes in non-educational settings – eg in police training, retail organizations, manufacturing industry, etc – have, in the past, been less likely to lead to accreditation. Their trainees usually have to find all the motivation they need in the intrinsic interest or relevance to their work of the materials themselves. This will sometimes be too much to ask, especially if, as often happens, the trainees are expected to study in their own time, don't really see why they should be studying at all and, if they must, would rather do so by attending a 'real' course.

When your learners are reluctant, and especially if your **support** system is not all you would wish, the prospect of an externally recognized qualification might just possibly make the study seem sufficiently worthwhile. (At least reluctant learners will gain a passport that might get them to a better place!) And, while they are learning, they might appreciate some of the benefits that arise from regular **assessment**.

Even if your trainees are keen already, why not consider the additional reward of a transferable qualification? If your programme is at professional level, perhaps a university will validate your courses. Otherwise, consider approaching a trade association or professional body or an awarding body for vocational qualifications.

You may find that you can improve your programme by building in some of the criteria expected by the outside body. And, besides getting credit for your learners, the programme itself (and staff who contribute to it) may gain in credibility on account of the outside recognition.

Activities—*learning by doing*

'Activities' are one of the sacred cows of open and **distance** learning. Here, the designers of learning **materials** are following a precedent laid down by an earlier generation of 'programmed learning' writers. What they do is intersperse their texts with frequent questions or exercises that supposedly get the **learner** to apply the ideas being discussed in the materials. The author usually provides immediate **feedback** that helps the learner decide how well they are doing. Such activities are usually distinguished from the text typographically – eg by use of symbols, colour, a change of typestyle or boxes for the learner to write in.

Such activities are more than a modish design feature – or they can be if handled properly. In competent hands they can help your learners, for example:

- understand and apply the ideas in the materials

- relate the teaching to their own experience and examples

- obtain information that the materials cannot provide

- practise towards important **objectives**

- monitor their own progress.

But if activities don't live up to their promise, learners will readily skip them. They will bother only with those that appeal to their personal sources of **motivation**. For example, 'Will it help me with my work?' 'Will it count for **assessment**?' **Assignments** and **projects** can be seen as activities writ large.

So, whether or not we are using specially written materials, getting the activities right is of prime importance in MBL. They can be the engine that powers the learning. On my workshops for course developers, I usually suggest that we shift our focus away from course **content** on to what we want our learners to *do* with it. I see this as essential for any kind of course, not just for those involving MBL. That is:

What sort of questions, problems, tasks, exercises and projects might enable learners to engage in a productive way with your subject? Which of these might they do at their desks and which might involve **practical work** elsewhere? Which can they do on their own and which will require them to work with other people? Which should be assessed? And how can we ensure that learners get satisfactory feedback?

Get the activities right and all else will fall into place.

Aims—*why bother with MBL?*

Why are you (or your organization) getting into MBL? There are many reasons for doing so. It helps to be clear about what yours are. Why? Because the kind of MBL system that might suit some aims will not always suit others. And because people are not always up-front about what their real aims are; so we may find ourselves confused and frustrated because we are working at cross-purposes with them.

Here are some possible aims. Which of them, if any, seem similar to yours?

- To attract more **learners** of the kind you have already.

- To attract learners who are not being catered for anywhere at present, eg those who normally benefit less than most from education and training.

- To provide for learners whose personal situations (eg living in remote areas or working shifts) make it difficult for them to attend conventional classes.

- To teach increased numbers of learners without comparable increases in staff.

- To provide a more rewarding learning experience for learners.

- To economize on scarce resources.

- To make the delivery of education/training cheaper, faster or more convenient for the organization.

Needless to say, an MBL system will work at its best only when all participants are agreed about its aims. If some people are chiefly interested in improving the quality of learning while others are chiefly interested in, say, cutting costs, they are likely to get in one another's way. This is not to say that both aims cannot be achieved at once. But it helps if everyone is clear and honest about where their true priorities lie. Don't be surprised, however, if you run up against hidden agendas and plain conflicts of interest, maybe even **resistance**. Not everyone will necessarily share your vision of MBL.

What *is* your vision of MBL? How does it relate to your organization's overall statements of mission and vision (if it has made any)? How does it compare with what the impartial bystander, judging by the way your organization actually implements MBL, might assume to be its aims and priorities? Any mismatches may suggest a need for further **consultation** and **briefing**.

Alumni—*a little help from our friends*

In recent years, a number of UK universities have discovered something their North American counterparts have known, and benefited from, for decades. That is, each of them has thousands of alumni.

What does alumni mean? According to my dictionary, the word means 'nursling or pupil' and comes from a Latin word meaning 'to nourish'. Thus the colleges and universities, having nourished the minds and spirits of the students who pass through them, can appeal to their graduates as alumni – and hope for a certain loyalty in return. And possibly support, or even donations.

'So what?', you may say. Or even, 'I know this already; but what's it got to do with promoting MBL?' Simply this: to promote MBL, especially if it is something of an innovation, you will need all the supporters and **champions** you can find. So look for your alumni. People who have themselves been nourished by MBL are that much more likely to speak up for it and encourage its use by other people.

They don't have to be alumni of your own organization. They just need to be alumni of MBL. So, out there among the people of power and influence in your organization – the managers, key committee members, opinion leaders, etc. In the UK, for example, where are the Open University graduates, the Open College diploma holders, the beneficiaries of courses from National Extension College, Rapid Results, Wolsey Hall, etc – those who have found MBL to be, for them, a good thing? They may be your champions.

Many of them may not yet have made the connection. They may not realize that you are talking of a form of learning similar to that from which they have benefited. So help them see the connection. Encourage them to encourage others in using the approach that they have found so beneficial. They may even become **mentors** or part-time **tutors**.

As well as turning alumni into champions you may also want to look for opportunities to turn potential champions into alumni. Can you help any of your local opinion leaders to satisfy any of their own (high-level) development or information needs by means of a materials-based learning approach? The hundreds of managers embarking on distance learning MBA courses every year would seem to believe that MBL might work for them. As alumni, they may become advocates of its use in training and developing their staff.

Anticipation—*the need to think ahead*

Setting up a materials-based learning project is a bit like sending a robot landing craft to a distant planet. Once the craft has landed, there is little you can do to help it cope with the possibly harsh conditions it encounters. Will it survive those conditions? Will it prove capable of doing the job it was sent for? This will depend on how well you *anticipated* the planetary environment and equipped your craft with the appropriate technology. There will be no human beings on board to make do and mend.

Likewise, materials-based **learners** may be on their own most of the time. Once started, they may not easily be able to ask someone what is expected of them from day to day. They may not be able to ask for explanations of **materials** that confuse them. They may not be able to get extra resources. They may meet problems that tempt them to abort their 'mission' – yet often these are problems we might have anticipated.

I once worked with a materials development team whose members resisted my attempts to get them to anticipate such problems on the grounds that: 'We've got to leave something for the **tutors** to do.' Of course, we need to provide a **support** service that enables learners to get help from tutors or others when they most need it. But this service will be busy enough even with the best designed materials. Even there, learners will have plenty of need for contact with tutors. The **economics** of MBL would be shattered if we routinely employed tutors to make good the known imperfections of the course materials. As my colleague Brendan Connors once remarked, that would be as wrong-headed as sending a leaking cruise ship to sea on the grounds that it's time we got some use out of the lifeboats.

So we need to find out as much as possible in advance about our learners and their situations and how they are likely to use our materials. This we can do by carrying out **needs analysis,** by **evaluation** of previous courses and by the **developmental testing** of our materials. By such means we may ensure that our materials are as suited to our learners' needs and situations as we can possibly make them.

To ensure that our support system is equally appropriate, we also need to know about our tutors – about their **images of learning/teaching** and their likely ability to respond to learners' needs. Some may benefit from **staff development**.

Through such anticipation we can avoid misusing the learners' and tutors' precious time and energy.

APL—*the assessment of prior learning*

What is your experience worth? You've graduated from the school of hard knocks or the university of life, but what have you got to show for it? 'Not a lot' would usually have been the answer until recently, or nothing much in the currency of education and training – no diplomas, licences, certificates, degrees, etc. No transferable **accreditation**.

And yet, people's experience – whether in paid jobs, leisure pursuits, or caring for homes, children and elderly or infirm relatives – has often enabled them to develop insights and abilities that are at least as much use in the world as those to be gleaned from years spent in classrooms.

Why should such experience – and the learning that has come from it – not be formally 'certified' in the same way as classroom learning? No reason at all, in principle. For example, the Empire State College (State University of New York) has been assessing mature students' experiential learning, and giving them credit towards a degree, for 30 years or more. In the UK also, some institutions have given learners with appropriate experience 'advanced standing' in their progress towards certain qualifications. And, for several years now in the UK, the assessment of prior learning (or experiential learning) has been a route towards getting one of the new National/Scottish Vocational Qualifications.

But why should APL concern people in materials-based learning? 'If they've already learned, they don't need our materials', you might say. But that's just the point. Many MBL systems do not take people's previous learning into account. Therefore, they may be expected to work with some **materials** they don't need, and spend time and money, seeking to develop a competence which they could demonstrate already. As a result they may feel bored or patronized and end up as **drop-outs**.

If your MBL is directed towards vocational qualifications, you will clearly need to find a way of checking out people's prior competence and helping them build on it. But even if it is not, you may want to consider whether you can get evidence of relevant competence from people in such a way that it might save learners from having to take certain parts of your programme before getting credit for it. Not only might it save them time, cash and frustration; but it might cut down your drop-out rate and also speed your 'throughput' of successful learners.

Appraisal—*a regular reminder*

What kind of **support** have you given your staff in their training and development recently? For example, have you:

- helped them identify their training needs or choose a suitable learning programme?

- helped them find time, funding or facilities to tackle the programme?

- taken a continuing interest in their learning, enabled them to talk with you about what they are learning and encouraged them in applying what they are learning in their work?

- done your best to ensure that all your staff are mutually supportive of one another's need to learn and develop?

And what have you been doing to satisfy *your own* learning needs?

Questions like those above might usefully be asked of every **line manager** at his or her annual appraisal. At present, many managers do not see training as part of their job. If it is not in their **job description**, then this is hardly surprising. Yet the line manager is a key figure in the success of MBL (or any other sort of learning) in the workplace.

If you are concerned with workplace MBL, what can you do to get managers' training and **staff development** responsibilities defined in job descriptions and appraised in reviews of their performance? The more you can do, the more you will raise the profile of MBL within the organization and improve the chances of it making an impact on people's lives.

Needless to say, however, you can't expect something for nothing. If you are asking managers to take on *extra* responsibilities, how will you make it worth their while? What **benefits** can you offer them? What **rewards**?

Staff working on MBL in colleges and universities might also expect the subject to be discussed at appraisal time. Too often they are appraised only in terms of their classroom teaching (and research). Unless their investment of time and effort in rethinking their courses, developing MBL materials and tutoring materials-based **learners** is on the agenda, it may not be properly rewarded.

Assessment—*sticks or carrots?*

Assessment is often the tail that wags the dog of learning. This is true for any sort of formal, organized learning – materials-based or otherwise. Even if your **learners** are studying largely out of interest or because they seek the competences your programme promises – rather than to qualify for some privilege or obtain some coveted **accreditation** – assessment can exert a huge influence on how and what they learn. And if your learners are learning merely because they are required to, then assessment may be the only means of ensuring that they do it seriously (or at all).

Learners are always pressed for time. There is rarely enough time to do everything required of them by their course, let alone by other aspects of their lives. So they are likely to look at the various elements of the course and ask: 'Are we being assessed on this?' Not surprisingly, they are likely to concentrate their efforts on whatever is being assessed and, to a greater or lesser extent, neglect the rest. As in most areas of life, it's the squeaky wheel that gets the grease.

Hence, it is important to ensure that our assessment focuses on the key course **objectives** (the competences we aim to help our learners develop) – even if other, less central ones would be easier to test. To use the words of Robert MacNamara (when president of the World Bank), 'We must strive to make the important measurable, rather than the measurable important.'

Learners often regard regular marked **assignments** as a valuable **pacing** device – to keep them at it when other pressures threaten to distract them. Furthermore, the **feedback** that **tutors** give them on such assignments may be vital in reassuring them that they are making worthwhile progress and in kindling their further learning.

But assessment in MBL systems can pose some special problems – especially if the learners are not known personally by the assessors, eg in distance learning. Are some aspects of learning difficult to assess at a **distance**? Can an assessment method that works fine with 50 students be scaled up to work with 500? Can you guard against **cheating**? Can you be sure whose work it is that you are assessing? Do you need **examinations** as well as coursework assessment? Is your assessment rigorous enough and secure enough to ensure the **credibility** of your system? Will the certification you award be recognized in credit transfer schemes?

Assignments—*a focus for learning*

Do your **learners** do courses? Or do they do assignments? Very often, whatever we offer in the way of a curriculum, learners see it terms of: 'What tasks do we have to do to get the credit/an acceptable grade/signed off/the certificate, or whatever?' Many Open University students, for example, on receiving the package of **materials** for a new course, will look first to see what will be required of them in the eight or nine assignments they'll be sending to tutors – and then plan their studies accordingly. That is, they are assignment-driven.

There is no harm in this if the assignments are well-devised. Indeed, if there are no assignments, or they are poorly thought out, then the learners' efforts may be misdirected, or never really engaged at all.

A well-devised assignments scheme can help your learners in several ways:

- Assignments can focus learners' attention on the key ideas and on the most important competences that the materials can help them develop. Thus, they can help your learners learn.

- Assignments may take the form of a mini-research **project** or some kind of foray into their own community or workplace that enables learners to adapt the pre-packaged learning material to suit their own local needs.

- If they form part of your **assessment** system, learners' assignments will be commented on (and maybe marked) by a **tutor** or other expert. Provided their tutors are willing and able to comment sensitively and supportively, the **feedback** can reinforce and extend the learners' learning.

- Feedback on assignments can promote **individualization**. That is, by getting their own work commented on, learners get responded to personally – as individuals, each with his or her own views, needs and concerns.

- For practical reasons, an assignments scheme usually has built-in **deadlines**. These help learners with **pacing** their studies. Knowing that they need to get an assignment in by a certain date will encourage them to keep up with their learning, even when other pleasures beckon.

What role might such assignments play in your MBL scheme? What benefits might they bring? What form might they usefully take? How frequent should they be? Who will assess them and provide the learners with constructive feedback on them?

Attitudes—*we've all got 'em*

You may already have found that mention of MBL reveals a range of beliefs, values and attitudes. Not all of them will be favourable to this 'new' approach to learning. For example:

- **Tutors** may say: 'What am I meant to do, if the **materials** are doing the teaching?' or 'Will I end up redundant?'

- **Learners** may say: 'I'd rather have time off work to go away on a real course' or 'It looks like the teachers are making me do their work.'

- Learners' **line managers** (in training contexts) may say: 'I didn't get where I am today by being spoon-fed' or 'I'm too short-staffed to give them time off for training.'

- Administrators may say: 'It doesn't fit the system' or 'It will be too difficult to control.'

- Potential sponsors may say: 'This looks like a cheap and second-rate substitute for real teaching.'

- The powers-that-be in your organization may say: 'Just think of all the money we'll save.'

Such **feelings** are not to be dismissed lightly. Ignore them and they can lead to **resistance** or to **failures** in your system. Even some experienced teachers, for example, may need help in making a major shift in attitudes if they are to work effectively in their new support roles – eg:

- from deciding what must be learned to helping the learner decide

- from conveying information to helping the learner learn

- from acting as the critical and impersonal expert to building relationships

- from using assessment to decide a grade to using assessment in order to help the learner learn (eg by written comments)

- from teaching face-to-face to teaching in writing or on the telephone

- from putting on a performance to nurturing a person.

It can be fatal to pretend that everyone in an organization feels similarly about MBL. It is healthier to get the different perspectives out in the open where they can be exposed to discussion and to evidence that MBL does have **benefits** that all can share in. The keys to successful change are usually **consultation** and **staff development**.

Benefits—*and the need to sell them*

Believe it or not, you'll meet people who don't see the point of MBL. Some will fear it, perhaps because they don't much like anything new, or because they suspect it may make life difficult for them. Others will simply pooh-pooh it as just the latest (and swiftly passing) educational bandwagon.

But you need these people's goodwill and co-operation. Otherwise you will meet **resistance** and MBL may come to a sticky end or never get started at all. One approach to overcoming unhelpful **attitudes** is to help colleagues to consider the possible benefits – for their learners, for their organization and for them as individuals. What might they hope to *gain* from MBL?

Here are a few suggestions for starters. We may be able to tell:

- potential **learners** that they will be able to study at a place, time and pace of their own choosing

- **tutors** that they will enjoy more stimulating relationships with learners and will themselves learn new and marketable skills

- **line managers** that they will get more productive staff with less training time spent away from the job

- administrators that they will get more opportunities to make their own decisions

- top managers that the scheme will contribute to the corporate 'mission'

- sponsors that they will be able to provide training for people who would otherwise not be able to take part.

As for your own organization as a whole, MBL may be the only means of finding enough new learners to keep your existing courses running and the existing staff employed.

Needless to say, you cannot afford to peddle empty promises. The benefits you propose must be realistic. Otherwise you'll live to regret making them!

Furthermore, you need to be willing to negotiate. The people you are trying to influence may want to influence you back. That is, they may want to sell you a few benefits you hadn't thought of – like the opportunity to contribute to shaping the policy for MBL in your organization. They may want to share in the **ownership** of the new approach. And they may expect enhanced **rewards** for their co-operation.

Briefing—*what are we meant to do?*

No doubt you know what you're meant to be doing. But do other people? MBL is constantly recruiting people who are new to it. We may easily assume that course development **teams** know what their **roles** are – that **learners** know what MBL will demand of them – that tutors and administrators know how MBL differs from the kinds they are familiar with – that **line managers** know how to **support** those of their staff who are training with MBL. But we could be wrong.

Many people won't know, for example:

- the general principles of MBL
- how your particular MBL programme is meant to work
- what demands it might be making on them
- examples of how these demands might be tackled
- the ways in which things might go wrong
- where to get help if they do.

We can't just leave people to pick up the knowledge (and **attitudes**?) as they go along. If an MBL programme is to be a success, we must introduce it carefully to all participants – not forgetting those who may join some time after the programme has got under way, eg new members of staff or the *next* cohort of learners.

Where possible, briefing might usefully include **face-to-face sessions**. These might include contributions from staff or learners who have worked on this or similar programmes before and can say what it's *really* like.

But most participants, learners or staff, will also need *written* guidance. Thus, for example, we might provide learners with **course guides**, specimen **examination** questions and answers, and reports from previous learners. Tutoring staff might need notes on how to mark **assignments** with samples of the kinds of **feedback** that learners find helpful. With work-based learning, we might need to provide line managers with notes about what the course is trying to achieve, about how they and the learners might benefit and about ways in which managers like them have been able to support such trainees in the past.

But briefing is not a one-off event. There is a limit to how much people can absorb up-front when starting something new. So be prepared to refresh the briefing from time to time (eg through informal chats, correspondence or computer **conferencing**). Briefing can shade into **staff development**.

Case studies—*learning from others*

MBL was not invented yesterday. Countless people have been this way before. There is no need for you to repeat all of their mistakes; nor need you miss out on some of their insights and useful stratagems.

The experience of many providers of MBL has been recorded in case studies that tell us what they were trying to do, how they set about it and what the outcomes were. Thus you can benefit from their experience. Knowing what worked well and what didn't (and why) may help you in designing your own MBL system.

Such case studies are to be found in places too numerous to detail. However, if you are interested in open, distance or flexible learning, look out for the free case studies and project reports published by the Department for Education and Employment (tel: 01709 888688 for the latest list) and keep an eye on journals like *Open Learning* and *Open Learning Today*. Also, if you have access to the **Internet**, try the free *DEOS News*. Send the message 'SUBCRIBE DEOSNEWS Your first name and surname' to 'LISTSERV@PSUVM.PSU.EDU'.

If you are interested in resource-based learning on campus, seek out the series of case studies produced by The Oxford Centre for Staff Development at Oxford Brookes University, Oxford OX3 0BP (see Gibbs in the Further Reading section) and those published by the Open Learning Foundation, 3 Devonshire Street, London W1N 2BA.

Case studies won't tell us everything we might like to know, of course. Especially in the current climate of competition for funding, few people are keen to inform the world about the less satisfactory aspects of their projects (even if their organization will let them) and outright failures rarely get reported at all.

You may find it worth keeping a file of relevant case studies and try to visit some of the organizations to see things for yourself. The successes of other organizations may help you in convincing your more doubting colleagues. Likewise, other users' failures (which you may have to read between the lines, or listen 'off the record', to detect) can help you in curbing people's over-optimism about what MBL can achieve. Either way, they will help you refine your own ideas and perhaps take heart from knowing you belong to a world-wide 'invisible college' of practitioners engaged in this continuously evolving approach to teaching and learning.

Centres—*somewhere to learn*

One of the problems that **learners** may have with MBL schemes (especially in distance learning) is finding somewhere to learn. Even with on-site MBL, space may be at a premium. In the overcrowded colleges and universities I know, there's rarely a seat free in **libraries** after 9 am. And in workplaces and offices all the space is likely to be devoted to the organization's core business rather than to training.

So, the success of your MBL scheme may very much depend on ensuring that learners have a place or places (let's call them 'centres') where they can use their **materials**, and meet with other learners as well as with **tutors** or other supporters. Here are some questions that may start you thinking about what kind of provision would be desirable and possible:

- What kinds of activity might you expect to happen at a centre? eg:
  - individual work with materials and/or equipment
  - **practical work** (eg in a laboratory or workshop)
  - one-to-one meetings between learners and tutors
  - group meetings with a tutor
  - meetings of **self-help groups** (without a tutor).

- What kind of space(s) will such activities need? eg:
  - what size of room(s) will be needed?
  - do you need both quiet rooms and 'talk rooms'?
  - how flexibly might these spaces be used?

- What materials and/or equipment will be needed to support the centre's activities? eg:
  - books and journals
  - resource packs
  - computers and software
  - photocopying facilities
  - overhead projectors, screens, whiteboards, etc
  - vending machines for drinks and snacks.

- What staff will the centre need and what will be their duties (eg booking in users, maintaining equipment, giving advice, security)?

- Are your learners easily able to come to one site or are they widely scattered and in need of several centres?

- Will you need to rent premises from other organizations?

- What costs will be involved in setting up the centres and in running them?

Champions—*'the friends of MBL'*

You can't be everywhere at once. You can't attend every meeting, say your piece at every committee or put your point of view in every formal or informal discussion in your organization that happens to get round to the subject of MBL. That's why we all need champions – people who will speak well of our work in places where it matters.

But champions don't just happen. They need cultivating. So how do we cultivate a group of people who are not only well disposed towards us but are also ready, willing and able to support us effectively?

There are four stages to this:

1 Identify those colleagues who are already well disposed or who could usefully become so. (The more influential they are as power-brokers or opinion-leaders, the better.)

2 Do all you can to make them aware of the **benefits** of your MBL projects and ensure they are kept up-to-date on how it is working out – both the triumphs and the problems.

3 Encourage them to share their understanding of your projects with colleagues (always alerting them to any occasions on which their support could be crucial).

4 Let them know that you appreciate the support they've been giving you.

Looking at point 1 above: Who might be your potential champions? Anyone who is working with you on your projects. Members of advisory groups. People outside your organization who 'have the ear' of influential people inside it. Colleagues who have benefited from MBL themselves (**alumni**), eg as Open University students. Your learners' mentors or **line managers**. Influential members of key committees. Don't let a likely champion go undetected.

As for 2 above, keep your champions up to date through regular **briefings**, **newsletters**, brief reports or computer **conferencing**, asking for their advice where appropriate and encouraging them to contribute to your projects, eg by **commenting** on **course specifications** or **materials**, and inviting them to any launch parties or celebratory get-togethers that your projects give rise to.

So, if MBL has met or is likely to meet any kind of **resistance** in your organization, you will now have a cadre of well-informed, enthusiastic allies to help you do battle with it.

Cheating—*and how to minimize it*

One of the little-mentioned problems of MBL is that you may not know your **learners** very well. In fact, you may not know them at all. You may never have met them, never spoken with them on the phone and have not the slightest idea what they look or sound like. All you have perhaps is their signature on an enrolment document and various pieces of work which you are meant to assess before you award them some kind of **accreditation**.

But was this work produced by the person who is registered for the course? If you think this won't be a problem because you'll be meeting the person who produced the work, be careful. In the UK, the chairman of the RAC recently reported that driving examiners estimate that as many as 1000 people a week 'pass' their driving test because an impostor has taken it for them. GCSE and A level exams may also have their annual crop of impostors and cheating is commoner than we usually admit in 'conventional' university courses. Why shouldn't it happen in your field also?

You can minimize the chance of such cheating by using some suitable combination of the following approaches:

- keeping the numbers per tutor small enough that you and your colleagues will know each learner personally

- requiring to see the passport of the person registered and issuing identity cards

- obtaining a specimen of the registered person's handwriting

- speaking to learners on the telephone about every assignment they produce for assessment purposes

- ensuring that the person registered for the course is interviewed face-to-face at least once during the course

- setting assignments that differ from learner to learner (and changing them from year to year)

- requiring learners to bring identity cards or passports to any **examinations** or other **assessment** exercises.

This may all sound rather paranoid. In a sense it is. You won't want to increase your costs and risk alienating your perfectly honest learners for the sake of what may be a non-existent threat – or almost. But the **credibility** of your MBL system might be severely damaged by even one or two well-publicized impostures. So how careful do *you* need to be?

Collaboration—*together we can?*

If you want to do the best for your **learners**, you may decide you can't do it alone. You may need to collaborate with other people. I don't mean working as a **team** with others inside your organization or using outside **consultants** – though this may be vital too. I mean working with outside organizations.

You might, for instance, want to collaborate in the areas of developing MBL **materials**, in delivering courses, in providing learner **support**, in **staff development**, in research or in course **evaluation**. Some random examples:

- The Open University produces and broadcasts its radio and television materials in partnership with the BBC.

- Eight separate Scottish police forces collaborate in developing shared materials that all their trainees can use.

- The National Extension College provides learners with materials and in-course assessment while numerous local colleges provide their **entry counselling**, learner support and end-of-course **assessment.**

- The Open University and other institutions often develop materials for their own students but have them produced and more widely marketed by commercial publishers.

- East Kent Tourist Board, the county council, small hoteliers and local colleges collaborate in developing and delivering a course on French for workers in the hotel trade.

- Numerous universities now deliver courses world-wide by **Internet, conferencing** and other media with learner support provided by local institutions.

Collaboration does, of course, mean that you will have to give up some of your autonomy. You may not be able to have everything exactly as you would have had it if you'd been on your own. But then again, you might not have had it at all if you'd been on your own. Collaboration may give you access to funding, learners, personnel and specialist expertise that would otherwise be unavailable to you. And your joint venture may proceed more quickly and achieve higher standards of **effectiveness** than solo efforts ever could.

But make sure your **aims** are compatible with those of your collaborators. Draw up explicit **contracts** about who is to do what. Be sure about how the **costing** and **benefits** are to be shared. Agree **quality** standards. And be extra vigilant with **monitoring** and evaluation.

Commenting—*like a 'critical friend'*

If you are one of a team developing learning materials, then you may sometimes need to play the role of critical friend. That is, you may need to offer constructive comments and suggestions about colleagues' **course specifications** and draft **materials**. If you are **managing** such a team, then you may need to suport colleagues in doing this for one another.

My experience in Open University course **teams** and elsewhere convinces me that commenting can make or break the quality of the materials produced. But good commenting doesn't always come easily. Here are some suggestions gathered from discussions with experienced critical friends:

- Comment on other people's work as you would wish them to comment on yours.

- Avoid seeming godlike in your commenting – we too are only human and our work will probably be as capable of improvement as the next person's.

- 'First the good news' – always look for something to comment on positively before you draw attention to things you are less impressed by.

- In general, try not to see materials in terms of good and poor aspects but in terms of good aspects and aspects capable of *further development* or improvement.

- If you think something could be improved, make sure you can offer a suggestion as to how.

- Don't overwhelm with criticism. Be selective. Focus on the main issues. How many new ideas can the author take on board in the time at his or her disposal?

- Remember you're helping your colleagues improve *their* materials, not the ones you would have written.

- Aim to leave the other person feeling understood, valued and invigorated by the attention you've given to their work, so that they will renew their efforts to make the best job they can of it. Don't leave them feeling so castigated and incompetent that they never want to look at it again.

- Don't say anything about a person's work behind their back that you wouldn't say to their face. Once they got to hear of it (and they would), they'd be unlikely ever to welcome your comments again.

- Avoid using red ink – we saw too much of that in school!

Communication—*keeping all in touch*

The success of MBL obviously depends on our being able to communicate with **learners**. But who else might you need to share ideas and feelings with in promoting MBL? Almost certainly your **team** members, perhaps **champions** elsewhere in your organization and maybe other people (inside or outside of the organization) who still need persuading about, or at least being kept in touch with, your MBL projects.

In the hurly-burly of getting an MBL project up and running, it is easy to forget the need to keep people well-informed (and well disposed). Such a 'task focus' can endanger the project.

Here are my suggestions as to how effective communication might be built into the running of an MBL project:

- regular **briefings**, updates and **debriefings**

- relevant documents – eg **course specifications**, publicity leaflets, course **materials**, etc – provided for all who might conceivably need them

- written guidance for colleagues on their various **roles** – both in general and in relation to a specific task

- a system for **commenting** sensitively on one another's materials or **support** activities

- regular **evaluation** or **feedback** sessions in which staff can air and compare experiences

- team meetings to which all staff (including secretaries, receptionists, technicians, etc) are expected to contribute

- regular **newsletters** in which colleagues can report experience, pass on tips, ask for people's reactions

- noticeboards on which colleagues can exchange ideas – and/or or use e-mail and computer **conferencing**

- informal gatherings – eg parties, lunches, visits to theatres or sporting fixtures – promoting 'social **glue**'

- regular chats, discussion and **consultation**

- a **quality assurance** system that picks up discontent

- representation for the project on all relevant committees.

You will no doubt have others you'll need to add. But don't forget that communication is a two-way process. You will have plenty of ideas and feelings to convey to other people; but the success of your MBL project may depend on how carefully you listen to what they are trying to convey to you.

Competition—*alternative attractions*

In one of my recent workshops for course developers, I asked the group: 'What do your **learners** read when they are not reading your course materials?' One person said (to groans of recognition elsewhere in the room): 'My learners don't read anything, they watch television!' Another capped this with: 'My learners don't even watch television, they play computer games.'

Well, that's what I mean here by competition. Not the alternative providers of MBL. Not even the alternative courses that learners might opt for within your own organization. These do need to be taken account of as part of your **market research**. But they are not likely to be overlooked.

What you are unavoidably competing with also – for your learners' time, **motivation**, and possibly money – are the alternative pursuits they might find attractive. They could be organizing their own informal learning, travelling more, exploring new job possibilities, taking up a new sport, joining a new club, doing voluntary work or even (last refuge of the desperate politician) spending more time with their families.

So what is the 'unique selling factor' that your MBL has to offer? In what ways might it be more satisfying for its own sake – eg in stimulating the learner's neglected talents? In what ways might it open a gateway to more satisfying outcomes – eg a better job (or any job)?

And what if they do choose your MBL? The competition is still the competition – waiting on the sidelines ready to commandeer your learners' time if you fail to match its satisfactions. How can you make your MBL **materials** as attractive and **user-friendly** as certain other leisure-time materials your learners might be enjoying if they were not spending their time studying? You may have problems matching the production qualities they take for granted in broadcast television. Unless you are using advanced **technology**, you may have trouble matching the **interactivity** that hooks them on computer games. How far can you go towards matching even the graphics, colour and editorial flair of the newspapers and popular magazines they voluntarily spend their money on every week?

The further you can go – without, of course, losing the integrity of what you are trying to achieve – the longer you are likely to hold their interest when the **workload** becomes onerous and competing pursuits begin to beckon.

Computerized testing—*pros & cons*

So-called 'objective tests' – the kind that lend themselves most easily to computerized marking – are more widely used in the USA than in the UK. And within the UK, they are used more in some areas of education and training – eg medicine and the Inland Revenue – than they are in most. Recently, however, the explosion in learner numbers – 'How can we find time to mark all these essays!' – has created new interest in tests that can be marked (and even presented to learners) by a computer.

There are two types of computer-marked tests:

1 those in which **learners** indicate their answers on printed forms – which are then scored by an 'optical mark reader';
and

2 those in which learners tap their answers directly into the computer system by means of a keyboard.

With 1 you are restricted to asking the traditional types of 'objective' question. You can invite the learner to *choose* one or more possible answers from several that are offered, to rank answers in some kind of order, to match items in one list with items in another,and so on. With 2 you can also ask open-ended questions (without sample answers to choose from), inviting learners to key in *their own* brief answers.

Possible benefits

- Setting progress tests for learners (numbers no object!) more frequently than would otherwise be practicable.

- Early warning of learners at risk of becoming **drop-outs**.

- Automatic contributions to vital **record-keeping**.

- Automatic **feedback** to learners – eg not just their overall score but also a printed discussion of the questions.

Possible snags

- Higher-level (creative) abilities are less easy to test.

- Writing effective questions is not quick or easy.

- You may need elaborate safeguards against **cheating**.

- With 2, learners need access to linked computers.

You might want to react to such snags by using computer-marked **assessment** only to aid learning and not allowing it to count (or only very little) for **accreditation**. But if it can stimulate learners' **motivation** and help you keep track of their progress you might find it still makes a worthwhile addition to the **effectiveness** and quality of your MBL system.

Conferencing—*learning together apart*

Scanning the US literature on **distance** education, you'd be hard put to know that **materials** might have anything to do with it. The emphasis there seems to be on three main ways of enabling **tutors** to talk with **learners** directly using the **technology** of tele-communications. These three ways are:

Video conferencing

This is based on some means of sending live video pictures and sound back and forth between two or more distant sites. Users at the two sites can see and speak to one another. The most common use resembles a traditional large-group **lecture,** except that most of the learners are not in the same location as the lecturer. But the medium can also lend itself to smaller group discussions and demonstrations.

Audiographics conferencing

Audiographics developed out of audioconferencing (a telephone conversation involving several people at the same time). It enables groups working on dispersed sites to talk to one another and to produce and exchange graphics (and other data) using their linked computer screens. If video cameras are added, users can also see one another on their screens.

Computer conferencing

Computer conferencing is a development of e-mail. Provided they have access to a computer linked to a central 'server' computer, learners and tutors can both send written messages to the rest of their group and pick up and reply to messages left by other members. This allows discussion among people who may *never* be in the same place at the same time.

All the above **media** allow **interactivity** of a kind that is not normally part of MBL. They can enable learners to share experience (thereby perhaps needing less material) and even to learn collaboratively. They can thus help lift the potential loneliness of the materials-based learner (and tutor).

With video conferencing and audiographics, learners and tutors can enjoy this interactivity only if they are willing to be in a certain place at a certain time. And this is to forfeit one of the valued freedoms of MBL. Computer conferencing, however, is 'asynchronous' – as with an exchange of letters, people will be 'speaking' to you when it suits their timetable but you can hear them and reply when it suits yours.

Might some form of conferencing enable certain **aims** or **objectives** that would otherwise be impossible for *your* MBL?

Consultants—*getting outside help*

We often can't do everything on our own. Even if we are working as a **team**, we may find we lack certain essential knowledge, expertise or experience – or simply the person-hours to get everything done in the **time** available to us. In such circumstances, we may need to recruit some temporary help from outside.

For example, Open University course development teams have always been ready to bring in academics from other institutions. The role of such persons has usually been to develop **materials** in some aspect of the course where the resident team lacked subject-matter expertise. Conversely, I am often called in by other institutions to provide **commenting** on their materials or **support** systems, to help with **staff development** or to carry out some **evaluation**.

Clearly there are potential benefits in this – flexibility, specialist expertise, extra prestige, lower salary overheads, the stimulus of a fresh viewpoint. But there are also potential snags. What are these potential snags, and how might we best overcome them?

The first potential snag lies in choosing your consultant. How can you be sure they are capable of delivering what you require? Get evidence of what they have produced previously or speak to people who have worked with them. Might it be worth providing staff development to help them acquire any additional competences they need for your project?

Secondly, most MBL projects involve working in teams. How do you induct your (probably part-time) consultant into the ways and expectations of his or her temporary colleagues? Here it can be helpful to have a team member 'adopt' the consultant, act as the official channel of **communication** and keep him or her up to date on what is going on.

Thirdly, many consultants, however keen, may be too new to MBL to know quite what they are letting themselves in for. In addition, they may have pressing responsibilities elsewhere. So make sure the consultant gets a thorough **briefing** and can be in no doubt about what is needed and by when. Then agree a **contract** that sets this out in writing and makes clear what will happen if either party is not satisfied.

Have a *substitute* consultant in mind in case your first choice fails to deliver. And consider whether **collaboration** with another organization might be a safer way of getting the extra expertise you need.

Consultation—*to win hearts and minds?*

Unless you are very fortunate, you won't be able to pursue MBL very far without considering other people's **feelings** and **attitudes**. For instance, you may already be wondering how to cope with a shortage of funds and staff and **institutional support**. Such constraints often ease appreciably if you can change people's perceptions of materials-based learning.

People's attitudes to new schemes can be unhelpful for a variety of reasons, eg:

- They haven't been consulted about what is proposed.
- They don't see why the scheme is necessary.
- They believe such schemes have failed in the past.
- They distrust the people who are proposing the scheme.
- Their cherished values seem threatened, eg 'We'll lose the human dimension' or 'The quality of learning will suffer.'
- They fear not being able to cope with new ideas or learn new ways
- They fear loss of status, security, money, time, influence.
- They fear they may be making themselves redundant.

Most of these reasons may stem from the first. Hence the need for genuine consultation. How might you overcome the fears and concerns of all those individuals and groups whose goodwill is necessary to the success of your scheme? How can you sell them the **benefits** of your scheme?

But consultation is a two-way affair. The object is not just to sell. You may be able to do more than persuade people of the virtues of your scheme. You may be able to get them to join in the **ownership** of it. In order to do this, they will need to have a share in making it. So let them see that their opinions are taken into account – eg get them to comment on plans, **course specifications** and **materials**, circulate their ideas, take up their offers of contributions, make sure your materials contain a printed acknowledgement of how they have helped. Consider getting them together occasionally (either in the flesh or by e-mail) as an informal advisory group. (Make sure it is well seeded with your **champions!**)

So there's more to be had from consultation than support and goodwill. You may also get some useful ideas and offers of practical help. And you needn't consult only people who have power over you. Sound out your wider **networking** contacts. Maybe you can use **conferencing** or the **Internet?**

Content—*a secondary consideration?*

Some would-be teachers and trainers seem to assume 'I've taught them, so they should have learned.' In other words, if they've told the **learners**, and especially if they've done so in print, then that's the limit of their responsibility. Anything more and they fear being accused of what they regard as the ultimate sin – 'spoon-feeding'.

But delivering the course content (however clearly) is *not* enough – either in 'conventional' teaching or in MBL. Why are we conveying this content? What do we intend learners to do with it? Not just memorize it, surely. More likely we want them to use it in attaining a variety of competences – intellectual, physical or inter-personal. The trick, therefore, is to get learners *interacting* with the content – and possibly developing content of their own, by exploring examples in their own experience (perhaps through **projects**).

This suggests we design the teaching around **activities**, **assignments** and **projects** that enable the learners to try things out and get **feedback** either from us or our materials or from other people. Without such structure, our content will remain inert on the page or screen. It will make as little impact as learners' **lecture** notes, dutifully written and filed away but never revisited. For similar reasons, it can be counter-productive to base MBL materials too closely on a teacher or trainer's lecture notes – unless, of course, the 'lecture' was one that required learners to do something more active than listen.

Problems often arise when course developers start out by saying: 'What content do I want to put across?' Too often there seems to be no end to the content that might be relevant. After all, other teachers might see this material and one doesn't want them to doubt the breadth of one's knowledge, does one? And one also wants to show that one is up there working at the leading edge of the subject, doesn't one? So courses often get packed out with content which the learner doesn't need and hasn't got time to read. First step on the road to **workload** problems and **drop-out**.

A more productive question to ask at the outset is: 'What is it appropriate for learners to *do*?' Begin, that is, by identifying learning activities that will help them develop towards the relevant **objectives**. *Then* you can ask: 'What content do I need to provide them with or help them find (and how?) in order to carry out and learn from these activities?'

Contracts—*getting it in writing*

Many MBL projects run aground because people weren't clear what they were responsible for or what they could expect of others. Such clarity is essential when working with outside contributors or in **collaboration** with other organizations.

For instance, more than one course has missed its launch date because **consultant** writers were late with their course **materials**. Why? Often because of loose agreements to pay their fee when (or if?) they hand over the final draft at some comfortably distant date rather than paying them stage by stage as they produce a sequence of acceptable drafts on time.

Contracts with course writers will need to cover:

- the **content** and **objectives** he or she is responsible for
- staged **deadlines** for hand-over of each draft
- **quality** standards for acceptability at each stage
- the fees payable at each stage (and penalties applicable)
- **copyright** responsibilities and ownership.

If you are recruiting people on a freelance basis to provide **support** for your **learners**, they too will need contracts, eg:

- What forms of support are they to provide?
- To what standards of quality?
- What determines the fees they are paid?
- What support (eg **staff development**) can they expect?

Similarly, collaborating *organizations* need to get their respective obligations and expectations clearly set down and agreed. Such collaborations often start up in an atmosphere of amicable euphoria but collapse into resentment and frustration later on because people disagree as to who was to have done what by when and to whose satisfaction.

Finally, what about the 'contract' between you and your *learners* (or **customers**)? Some sort of contract always exists, even if no one has spelled it out. It covers what might be learned (objectives and content), how the teaching will be done, **assignments** required, standards and criteria to be used in assessment, support and facilities to be provided, timetables, and so on. What do you expect from the learners? What can they expect from you? Future complaints may be avoided by discussing such matters with your learners and/or setting down the main points in writing for both sides to agree.

Copyright—*your permission to reproduce?*

MBL relies on **materials**. Any material anyone produces is copyright material – even a shopping list or a home video. Someone, usually the person who created it, or paid to have it created, owns that copyright. If you want to reproduce any of that material, you need the owner's permission. They may or may not be prepared to give you 'clearance'. If they do, they are entitled to ask for a fee, which may be substantial.

Making mistakes in this area can turn out to be costly. Even if it doesn't involve you in court cases, it can still result in last-minute, unplanned-for demands on your budget. In the worst case, you might have to pulp your learning materials.

If you are simply planning to buy multiple copies of the materials to include in your learning package, then there is no problem. You may even negotiate a useful discount.

The problem arises when you want to either:

1 reproduce extracts (eg paragaphs, diagrams, video clips) from other people's materials in materials that you are developing, or

2 reproduce the complete work (eg an article or book chapter or video-tape) and provide multiple copies for your learners.

As far as 1 is concerned, permission may not be needed for a small extract from a lengthy text. But, to be safe, I would suggest you seek permission for *anything* you want to use (especially from non-print media). Write to the copyright owner (usually via a publisher) as early as possible, telling them exactly what parts of their material you want to use (eg give page numbers or send a copy) and the context in which you plan to publish it – eg form, number of copies, internal use or generally available, free or priced, etc. Make it as easy as possible for them – eg send them a stamped envelope and a standard letter confirming permission which they may simply sign and return.

As far as *print* in 2 is concerned, many UK organizations in education or training have taken out a blanket licence with CLA (the Copyright Licensing Agency, tel: 0171 636 3745). Find out what this entitles you to reproduce in your situation. If your organization is not covered, proceed as for 1 above.

Two final questions: Does *your* organization have a specialist who can advise you and seek copyright 'clearance' on your behalf? Are copyright fees fully allowed for in your budget?

Correspondence teaching—*is OK!*

For the last couple of years, I've been immersed in a form of teaching and learning that brings a whole new meaning to corrspondence education. I've been spending several hours a week reading messages from learners to me and to one another and sending them messages in reply. We have all learned a lot in the process, thanks to the intense **interactivity** and the **feedback** we've all enjoyed. We've been computer **conferencing** – and computer conferencing I see as correspondence teaching 'with knobs on'.

You'll often hear people sneering at old-style correspondence courses – the first wave of **distance** learning. But good correspondence courses had one vital component that has sometimes been downgraded or overlooked altogether in more recent MBL courses – ie *correspondence*. It was never enough for students to grind away at **materials**. They also had to keep in touch with a **tutor** by correspondence, and maybe by telephone. They could get tutors to respond to their concerns and their problems. And they would be expected to complete regular **assignments** and mail them off to their tutors who would return them with marks and helpful comments. This would help **individualize** their learning and also help reassure them that they were making reasonable progress. Whatever their shortcomings may have been in the quality of **materials** provided, such systems did at least highlight for us the other side of the coin – **support**.

Admittedly, in the 160 years since Isaac Pitman began teaching shorthand by mail, correspondence education has had a mixed press. It has attracted a fair few rogues and low-value providers as well as numerous excellent institutions like the UK-based National Extension College and International Extension College.

Several large and respected universities, especially in the USA, still offer correspondence study as well as their on-campus programmes. There are many respectable commercial correspondence colleges in a variety of countries that enrol millions of students a year on well-presented and effective courses. And the US military also enrols millions of learners annually, making the Department of Defense the largest single 'correspondence college' in the world.

So, if anyone suggests to you that your MBL smacks of correspondence study (and is thereby inferior), don't let them escape with so cheap and ignorant a smear. Just ask them how much 'correspondence' (ie personal interaction with a tutor) their own on-campus learners are getting.

Costing MBL—*where will the funds go?*

MBL shifts the **economics** of teaching from low-cost preparation with high-cost delivery towards high-cost preparation with low-cost delivery. With MBL, we commonly expect relatively high fixed costs – getting the **materials** together, but relatively low variable costs – the costs per **learner** enrolled.

Your *fixed costs* are those that do *not* depend on how many learners you enrol. In fact, many of them are incurred before you enrol any at all. They may include the costs of:

- **market research** and publicity
- salary costs of:
  – developing the course materials
  – **staff development**
  – **developmental testing** of the course
- payment for **copyright** permissions
- salaries of any managers or **support** staff that must be paid regardless of how many learners are enrolled
- fees to **consultants** and outside suppliers
- premises (**centres**) and equipment needed for course
- course-related warehousing, transport, rent, rates, heating, telephone, insurance, etc
- contribution to the organization's general overhead
  – eg administrative staff salaries, use of premises and equipment, telephone, paper, postage.

Your *variable costs* are those that depend on how many learners you enrol. Each extra learner may cost you for:

- a set of the course materials
- any individual equipment or facilities you will provide
- individual support costs (eg salary costs of **tutors**, **mentors**, assessors, etc)
- **briefing** and staff development of support staff
- administration (eg **record-keeping**)
- lost production time (if you are the learners' employer).

Whether your course can at least 'break even' will depend on what fee your learners (or their sponsors) are willing to pay and how many you can expect to enrol. You'll need enough learners to ensure that the difference between their total fees and total variable costs will cover your fixed costs – unless creative **accountancy** can help you close the gap.

Course guides—*so what's it all about?*

Many conventional courses give **learners** very little information about what the work will offer them or demand of them. Perhaps we assume they'll pick up the ethos and the 'house rules' informally during their daily contacts with tutors and other learners. We can't make that assumption with MBL. Learners don't have many of those informal contacts. If we want them to know what the course is all about (and we do, don't we?) then we need to spell it out.

Maybe you can get your learners together for a **briefing** at a **face-to face session** before the course begins. That would be helpful (not least for spreading some 'social **glue**') but there's a limit to how much learners can absorb about a course before they've begun to study it. Hence the need for a **user-friendly** manual they can refer to later on – the course guide.

A course guide might include many kinds of information, including the following:

- an overview of the main themes or concerns of the course and why the course **team** think them important

- who the course is aimed at and what **prerequisites** and **images of learning/teaching** the team have in mind

- the aims and **objectives** of the course and of each section within it

- a detailed **contents** outline of the course

- a timetable or flow chart showing the **structure** and sequence, including **deadlines** and other critical events

- a description of the course **materials** learners are given

- details of further material they need to obtain themselves, eg annotated reading lists or sample **Internet** (Web) sites

- advice on how to study the materials, use any necessary equipment and make the most of the the **support** system

- a glossary of key terms

- details of how the **assessment** system works, including all course work **assignments** and notes on how to tackle them

- sample **examination** questions and details of the criteria that will be used in assessing learners' responses

- if you're brave, reviews from former learners about 'how the course really works'!

And course guides are not just for learners. *Staff* may also find them useful – especially if they help to write them.

Course specification—*spelling it out*

If you want to get funding to develop an MBL course or to develop one in **collaboration** with another organization, you may need to produce a detailed course 'specification'. This will also help you in producing a **course guide**. Here is what it might usefully include:

Preliminary

- Title of course.

- Overall **aims** of course. (How will the course contribute to the needs of the **learners** and/or the organization?)

- Perceived need for course. (eg was it suggested by potential learners or clients or confirmed by **market research**?)

- Approximate learning time in hours/weeks? (Is it realistic to assume that learners will have this amount of time to spare?)

The learners and their needs

- Intended learners. (What do we know of their characteristics and needs that might influence the design of the course?)

- Circumstances in which learners will be using the course. (eg at work or at home, with what access to equipment and other people who can help them?)

Objectives and content

- **Prerequisites**. (What experience/knowledge/skills will be required of learners *before* starting this course?)

- **Objectives**. What do we want learners to be able to *do* (or do better) as a result of working through (a) the course as a whole and (b) each unit or section within it?

- **Content** and sequence. (What are the main topics, themes or issues to be dealt with in the course? Can we give titles and content outlines for sections or units within it? In what order will the learner work through them?)

Teaching and assessment

- Teaching **media**. (Which media will be used – eg print, audio, video, computer **conferencing**? What will be role of each?)

- Learning **activities**. (eg What will learners be *doing* in typical learning sessions? How will the course aid them in this?)

- Human **support**. (What help must be provided for learners – eg by **tutors**, **mentors**, librarians, **line managers**, etc?)

- **Assessment**. (How will the learners' performance be assessed? By whom? At what stages during the course?)

Credibility—*keeping your image intact*

There is an old Czech joke to the effect that a cuckoo is just a nightingale that learned its singing from a **correspondence** course. That attitude is far from dead. Whether you are in education or in training, you will know that some people – eg colleagues, funding bodies, clients, potential **learners**, learners' employers, sponsors – are sceptical about MBL.

You may have to prove to them that MBL is not a second-rate substitute for 'real' courses. If you don't convince them, you won't get the funding, the staffing or the enrolments you need. So what might you need to do to establish the credibility of your MBL?

The UK Open University faced just this problem when we set up more than 25 years ago. (We were the first MBL university *and* we were recruiting 'unqualified' students!) We made a number of decisions then that no doubt helped establish our credibility. Maybe you'll need to do something similar in your situation. Here is what we did.

- Got ourselves a Royal Charter like any other university.

- Recruited our full-time staff and a network of part-time **consultants** and **tutors** from established universities.

- Set up various advisory bodies and steering groups to ensure that relevant 'interested parties' from outside were aware of what we were doing and could influence it.

- Cultivated various professional bodies (eg psychology, engineering, social work) to ensure that our courses would meet their requirements for membership.

- Contracted with established universities to run our summer schools on their campuses every year.

- Set up **teams** to develop courses and had the **materials** assessed by prestigious academics from other universities.

- Systematically and publicly evaluated all our courses.

- Assessed our students with both continuous **assessment** and **examinations**, which were moderated by an 'external examiner' just like any 'conventional' university.

- Began a public relations campaign (continuing still) to raise people's awareness of MBL and the achievement of our students and their acceptability to employers.

We also did something in the quest for credibility that I would *not* recommend – we put far too much **content** in many of our courses and gave students too heavy a **workload**.

Customers—*or our partners in learning?*

Colleagues in several universities have recently been outraged at the suggestion that we should regard our students as customers. I suspect that many trainers will be equally vexed at similar suggestions about their trainees.

I can understand their consternation. Students have traditionally occupied a deferential role in the educational hierarchy. Normally they have been younger than their teachers, less confident socially and have come from a learning **milieu** in which they have been relatively subservient to schoolteachers. They have known little of the ways of the world, let alone the subject they are studying and, by definition, need their teachers to decide what they should be learning. Moreover, their studies have been paid for by other people, so they may have felt on shaky ground protesting about less-than-adequate provision – even if they were willing to risk victimization for doing so. Much of this will apply to a considerable proportion of trainees also.

But things have changed. Students have aged. There are now many more 'mature students' in higher education, **learners** with more experience of the world than many of their teachers and only too aware of what they are sacrificing (their own money, their precious time and even perhaps their existing jobs) in order to be students. They (and their younger, often impoverished colleagues) will often expect to help decide what and how they are to learn – and to kick up a fuss if what they see as their **needs** are not respected. Can we wonder that learners are now applying 'value for money' criteria to educational provision – just as they would as customers or clients for any other professional service?

If we are to make MBL work, we need to respect learners' **attitudes**. Traditionally, both higher education and training have been driven by the producers' expectations rather than by the users' wishes. We have done things *to and on behalf of* our students or trainees, rather than *with them* and in response to their preferences. They have worked for us rather than we for them. Rarely has the traditional curriculum allowed much room for negotiation. In this respect, learners have often been treated like punters rather than as our *partners* in developing their learning. But MBL enthusiasts usually embrace such notions as choice, **flexibility** and learners taking active, critical responsibility for their own learning. Maybe the notion of learners as customers or clients can help us work together more collaboratively in meeting (while helping redefine) their needs?

Deadlines—*helping people stay alive*

Deadlines don't sound very **user-friendly**, do they? Nor do cut-off points or even hand-over dates. But for many **learners** they will make all the difference between their staying in your programme or becoming **drop-outs**.

Materials-based **learners** are, by definition, likely to spend less time than most in contact with their teachers. Perhaps they will also spend far less time in contact with other learners. So they may miss many of the social cues that keep us applying ourselves when we are working closely with other people. If they are new to MBL, they may also lack some of the **study skills** – especially time-management skills – that are so essential to keeping up with the **workload**.

Part-time learners are particularly at risk. Apart from the factors mentioned above, they may face pressing distractions from the real world. Jobs, families and social life clamour for priority status. Studies can easily be allowed to drift.

Hence the need for deadlines – set dates by which learners are expected to *do* something. These may be the dates by which they are to get certain **assignments** to their **tutors** or when they are to present their ideas at a **face-to-face session**.

We may have qualms about setting too many fixed deadlines if one of our aims is to fit in with the circumstances of our learners. But the deadlines can, of course, be ones that we agree with each individual learner. We can also be **flexible** and renegotiate them if a learner runs into difficulties.

As teachers and trainers, we too are having to get used to deadlines of our own. We can no longer say, 'I'm working on these handouts and I hope to get them ready in time for the course.' If we don't get our **materials** ready, the course won't run. We can no longer use our charm and physical presence to make up for lack of course materials. If we don't meet our deadlines we may lose the respect of our peers, perhaps the custom of our clients and maybe even a good deal of money.

Hence, for example, the need for **scheduling** in materials development and for **contracts** that clearly say when authors are expected to hand over each draft of their material for **commenting** by other members of a **team**. Likewise, tutors may be expected to respond to learners with comments on their assignments within a given number of days.

I know that my efforts become more productively focused if I have a deadline. How about you and your learners?

Debriefing—*what was it all about?*

So what was it all about? What did we learn from it? Where do we go from here? These are the kinds of questions we might discuss with our **learners** after they have completed a learning programme – or a module within it.

Just as it is usually necessary for learners to have a **briefing** before they begin, it can be helpful to debrief them afterwards. Otherwise, it is only too easy to tick off the experience from their list of things to be done and throw all their thoughts and energies into getting on with the *next* challenge.

The danger of pushing on regardless is that learners may fail to reflect properly on that previous experience. As a result, they may be trying to move ahead with aspects of the course still undigested or misunderstood. This may imperil their later learning or hinder them in applying what they have learned to their work. And that may undermine what you are trying to achieve with MBL.

How can we help them reflect on their learning? The traditional, rather heavy-handed approach has been to have them sit a final **examination** under controlled (and stressed) conditions. More sensitive approaches might be to use **projects** or to have them report on their experience to their peers or to engage in a debriefing discussion with a **mentor**. Apart from anything else, such discussion should remind them that someone *cares* about their learning. (One police officer told me how he began valuing the distance learning **packages** he is regularly issued with only when his sergeant took to quizzing him and his colleagues about what they had learned.)

Furthermore, you may agree that we too (the course developers and providers) need to set aside time to debrief ourselves on completion of a project (or of stages within it). This can play an important role in our **staff development**.

Before we heave a collective sigh of relief and rush off to our next project, we might discuss: What has each of us learned? What has the **team** learned? How might it affect our future decisions or actions? Does it suggest any immediate staff development needs? Who cares about *our* learning? What more might we welcome by way of **institutional support**?

Definitions—*what sort of learning?*

What do you call your kind of MBL? If you are working in a system that's already established, it's name will be also – open learning, **distance** learning, resource-based learning, flexible learning, **technology**-based learning or whatever.

But what if you are just setting up? It is tempting to go for the name that's flavour of the month. Maybe you hope to benefit from whatever hype and funding that name has attracted. But beware of getting pinned down by labels that can soon become tarnished or outdated. Whichever of the many MBL 'brand-names' labels we go for, they will be liable to mislead or alienate as many people as they win over.

Here, in case you are interested, are my definitions of the four brand names that are most popular in MBL at present:

Open Learning is a *philosophy* – one of giving **learners** more *access* to learning and more *choice* and *control* over what and how they learn. Sometimes this means merely that learners are able to choose the 'time, place and pace' of their learning. But it can extend to opening the learning to new kinds of learners and giving them choice about what and how and with whom they learn. It may or may not involve **materials** or 'distance learning'.

Distance learning is a *technology* – one that enables learners to learn without being in the same place as their teacher, eg with the aid of specially prepared learning **packages** (or other materials that learners can acquire), **conferencing** and **correspondence** with a distant tutor. It may be no more 'open' than 'conventional' courses.

Resource-based learning is also a *technology* – one that enables learners to learn on-site with less direct help from a teacher but usually with frequent or extensive interaction with other learners. It may use specially prepared learning materials or simply collections of existing material together with a **study guide**. (It may be no more 'open' than 'conventional courses'.)

Flexible learning – can be any combination of the above, plus whatever other ingredients you feel like throwing into the pot! Possibly the most liberating of all the above labels, if you must have one; but none of them can compare with:

'Effective learning' – a learning system that uses the most appropriate *combination* of **media** and approaches (ancient and modern) to meet the needs of the learners you have enrolled.

Developmental testing—*or 'piloting'*

Most manufacturers will try out a new product before launching it on a wide scale. Film producers, for example, will often try out more than one pilot version of the same film – and put together the final version in the light of the **feedback** they get from early viewers.

'So what?' you may say: they are merely looking to maximize the popularity and profitability of their product. We, on the other hand, are more interested in 'learnability' and educational or training **effectiveness**. But we too – and our **learners** – may benefit by piloting our product (**materials** plus **support** services) on a pilot group of learners.

However experienced we are and however insightful our **anticipation**, we can never expect to foresee all the difficulties that learners are likely to have with our courses. Pilot learners' reactions may reveal a number of errors or design faults that we can put right before launching a course on its first run.

Here is the ideal form of developmental testing.

- Get a number of learners (preferably 20+, but half a dozen is better than none at all) to work though your materials (including **assignments** and tests, where appropriate) in as near as possible 'realistic working conditions'.

- Provide them with a **tutor**, a **help line**, meetings with other learners, back-up from their **line manager**, or whatever other kind of support is appropriate.

- Get them to fill in log-sheets during their work and/or complete questionnaires afterwards.

- Analyse the log-sheets, questionnaires, test results, etc.

- Discuss the course with a group of your pilot learners if possible (and with their supporters, if any).

- Identify the key weaknesses that have been revealed in your course and improve it in time for its first true run.

The above ideal is not always possible. You may be too short of time, you may be unable to find enough learners (or a means of persuading them to do the work for you) and 'realistic working conditions' may be impossible to set up.

Hence, pre-launch, you may have to rely on **commenting** from colleagues and a few learners. You will then need to regard your *first run* of the course as a developmental testing run – and hold back money (and staff **time**) in your budget to make perhaps major revisions before the course has its second run.

Distance—*who's distant from what?*

Beware of equating materials-based learning with distance learning. Not all distance learning needs to rely on **materials** (see computer **conferencing**) and much MBL takes place on campus or in the workplace where **tutors** and other **learners** are probably within easy reach.

That said, most materials-based learners are indeed likely to feel themselves more distant than 'conventional' learners – or at least more distant than conventional learners *used to* feel, before the recent worsening in student-staff ratios. One of my sons recently took a three-year degree course, as a mature student, at a well-established campus university. By the third year, and down to three hours of contact time per week, he said he felt 'like a distance learner but without the distance learning materials'. And, having previously done several Open University courses, he knew just what he was missing.

But what might materials-based learners feel more distant from? And what might we do to ensure their learning doesn't suffer too much on account of such **feelings**?

There is often some element of distance even with on-campus or workplace MBL. Which of the following might *your* learners feel they are not having enough contact with?

- the teachers/trainers who developed their programme

- someone who can respond to their individual concerns or difficulties (eg a tutor or **mentor**)

- the people who will assess their learning for **accreditation**

- other learners with whom they might pursue joint learning in a mutually supportive **milieu**

- equipment or facilities that might aid their learning

- the context in which, or 'clients' with whom, their learning is meant to be applied (eg student school teachers learning in college rather than among children in school).

Is there a *key* factor among those I've listed? I suspect that most learners' sense of distance (or isolation) depends chiefly on how quickly and satisfactorily they can get **individualized** help or **feedback** from another human being whose viewpoints seem relevant – eg a teacher, an assessor, another learner or co-worker or even a 'client'.

So how can you help *your* learners get such human **support**?

Diversity—*and how to cope with it*

Students and trainees are not what they were. They are more different – not just as a group but also among themselves.

In post-secondary education, students are no longer all much the same age, with similar educational backgrounds, experience of life and expectations about learning. Opening up **access** has greatly widened the age range, with mature students often working alongside those young enough to be their grand-children. Many of these will be older than their **tutors**, perhaps with greater practical experience in the subject of their studies and maybe with uneasy **feelings** about the learning situation in which they find themselves.

Likewise, changes in school curricula and more **flexible** entry requirements have made students' level of preparedness for courses much more variable. For example, even relatively 'traditional' universities find that they cannot rely on all science-based students having the high level of competence in basic mathematics that was once taken for granted.

The mixture of competence levels is augmented by the trend towards modular courses. These bring students together from a variety of programmes, with different backgrounds, different needs and different learning paths to follow after whatever module they are working on together at present.

Such increased diversity can also be found among trainees in industry and public sector organizations like the Inland Revenue, the police service and the National Health Service. The pressures from continuous external and internal change mean that employees of very mixed backgrounds, age and seniority are constantly in need of updating on the latest legislation, policy and procedures.

Both in education and training it becomes difficult to deal with a body of **learners** as if they were a homogenous mass. Traditional **lectures** have only a limited use. Different learners may need to start at different places, learn at different **paces**, follow different learning routes and use different approaches and **media**. They will also need plenty of **support** from tutors who can help them adapt the programme to suit their individual needs.

This may be exactly why you are using MBL – meeting individual needs by exploiting its flexibilities. But not all MBL systems allow for sufficient **individualization**. Does yours?

Drop-outs—*let's understand and explain*

It used to be rumoured that mustard companies made most of their profits from the surplus left on the sides of people's plates – and that drop-outs served a similar function in **correspondence** education. If that were ever true in the latter case, it certainly isn't true of MBL today. There is no benefit to be had, financial or otherwise, from **failure**.

Students and trainees often do fail to complete a learning programme on which they have embarked – or else delay its completion way beyond the time span that most of their peers spend on the programme. Even in 'conventional' universities – where MBL is not a factor – more and more undergraduates fail to complete their degree programmes.

Such students and trainees are often said to have dropped out. They may, however, have done so for a variety of reasons, eg because:

- the programme content does not meet their **needs**
- the programme approach does not suit them
- they've already got all they need from the programme
- the demands of job or family leave insufficient time for the programme
- they can't afford to continue with the programme.

One of my friends, for example, counts as a drop-out in Open University statistics because he took three courses and then no more. But that experience encouraged him to go on to do a first degree at another university and an MA at a third. Really he is another unrecorded *success* for the OU.

We must do what we can to *understand* the causes of whatever drop-out we are getting. We must do what we can to *prevent* drop-out of the kind that represent failure. And, if we want to present our results in the best possible light, we should try to tell the story of those who have got all they need from the programme without completing it.

How might your **record-keeping** identify people who are liable to drop out of *your* programmes or who have already done so? How might you find out *why* – eg something in the programme, something in them, something in the rest of their lives? Is there anything you can afford to offer them by way of extra **support** or encouragement if they might want to stay involved in learning or come back to it at a later date?

Economics—*comparative costs of MBL*

Don't assume that MBL will be learning on the cheap. How its economics compare with those of 'conventional' learning will depend on such issues as what kind of **materials** are used, whether they've had to be specially developed, who pays for them, what equipment and facilities are needed and how many **learners** are involved. (See also **costing MBL**.)

For example, developing a CD-ROM **package** for a small group of learners may be far more costly than providing those learners with a series of classroom sessions. On the other hand, if the number of learners increases greatly or if the package consists simply of print, then the MBL approach may be cheaper per learner than conventional classes.

The supremely cheap option would be large numbers of learners learning at home in their own time from material they have acquired at their own expense (or which you have managed to buy at a huge discount because of the large numbers involved) and without any **support** from **tutors** or other people who expect to be paid for their services.

At the other extreme, you might be providing for a handful of learners learning in their firm's high-rent premises, on full pay (taking time out from production), using a specially developed computer-based multimedia package, supported by their **line manager** (who also needs to take time out from production) and a tutor from a local college.

Despite that, it can still be financially worthwhile. Such expensive learning may still be cheaper than the only available alternative. Indeed, perhaps because people are working shifts or are spread all over the country, there may be no alternative. Added to which, the results may be *better* than those of any other form of learning. They may so add to quality or output, or save costs elsewhere, that their cost-effectiveness is unchallengeable.

In my experience, the most effective MBL programmes – both in education and in training – have not been developed to save money. Rather their aim was to provide **access** for learners who might otherwise be deprived of tuition – or simply to maintain or improve the **effectiveness** of learning.

So, don't encourage dreams of massive cost cutting. *Perhaps* you will save on running costs during presentation of the course (compared with conventional ones). But any such **economies** may be more than used up in advance – during the much more costly phase of course *development*.

Economies—*getting more for the money*

Many of us are weary of the relentless passion for cost-cutting that has driven public policy in recent years. Yet we all want to make optimum use of whatever funds we have available. What we spend on one thing is not available for spending on others. So, if we find we can spend less on one, we should (in theory) be able to spend more on something else.

This is as true in MBL as elsewhere. The more we spend on developing a course, the fewer courses we can develop. The more we spend on **technology**, the less we have available for more basic **media.** The more we spend on **materials**, the less we have available for **support**.

So where can we economize in providing MBL? Where can we cut costs without cutting **quality** – and thereby perhaps make resources available to improve quality in other areas? Here are some suggestions to start with:

- Buy in and customize other organizations' courses rather than developing your own from scratch.

- If you must develop your own, simply write a **study guide** to **existing material** (eg published texts and videos).

- Develop your course (and share costs) in **collaboration** with another organization.

- If you are considering using expensive technology and teaching media, ask yourself what benefits you might be able to provide for **learners** if you spent the money in other ways.

- Rather than giving all learners all materials (and maybe equipment), consider a leasing or buy-back scheme.

- Where your learners can work in groups, provide sets of materials to be shared rather than individual copies.

- Help learners develop the skills to find and use existing materials, eg in **libraries** or on the **Internet**.

- If learners have access to appropriate computers, put some of your materials on a database for them to download as they choose (rather than giving everyone everything).

- Where possible, have support provided by part-timers paid 'per student', rather than by full-time salaried staff.

- Lessen the load on **tutors** by spending time developing 'free' forms of support like **self-help groups** and **mentors**.

What suggestions can you add to this list? How might you optimize the use of resources in *your* MBL system?

Entry counselling—*a wise welcome*

Much failure in education (and to some extent in training) stems from the fact that **learners** have embarked on the wrong programmes. Undergraduates are often aggrieved to find that psychology turns out not to be about understanding people, while medical students often decide their chosen discipline is too much about people. And a 1994 report in the UK by OFSTED and the Further Education Funding Council (*16–19 Guidance*) expressed alarm at the number of A-level and vocational courses with a failure rate of 30–40 per cent. Poor quality of course provision accounted for much of this; but so too did lack of adequate guidance or entry counselling.

So it is easy to choose courses or programmes that turn out not to be what one expected or needed. If you are to minimize your **drop-outs** (and save your learners from wasting time and effort), you may need to find ways of helping prospective learners make realistic decisions.

Exactly what surprises might learners be letting themselves in for with *your* course or programme? What might they need to know in order to help them decide whether it is really for them? For example:

- Will they be happy with the **content**, level and approach?
- Can they afford the course (both money and time)?
- Have they got whatever **prerequisites** the course demands? (If not, can they be helped to get them?)
- Will they be able to cope with the **workload**?
- Will they have access to any necessary equipment or facilities?
- Will they need to travel anywhere or spend time away from home?
- Will they be comfortable with the **assessment** system?
- Will they be able to retake any assessments they fail?
- What **support** will they get, and from whom?
- What do previous learners say about the course?

Some such questions you may be able to answer by providing printed materials – eg detailed course outlines, sample **assignments** or **examination** questions, and critiques from previous learners. But you may also need to provide a **help line** or give potential learners a chance to meet with **tutors** or learners who have already been through the course.

Effectiveness—*where's the evidence?*

We can't take the effectiveness of materials-based learning for granted. Even if it generally achieves results that are as good as 'conventional' approaches, will it do so in your particular MBL project? And what does it all **cost**? You will want to know this and so, most likely, will whoever provided you with the necessary funds and encouragement to get it going.

So, in carrying out an **evaluation**, you may need to collect evidence of the following kinds:

- how many **learners** survive the course (see **drop-outs**)
- how learners are performing on non-MBL courses they have taken just before or at the same time as yours
- learners' results on **assignments, projects**, in-course tests and end-of-course **examinations**
- learners' performance in external professional examinations
- learners' acceptability to professional bodies or employers
- how well learners do in courses they go on to after yours
- learners' rates of progress through the course/programme
- comments made by external assessors about the quality of the teaching and learning
- learners' comments
- comments from **tutors**
- comments from work-based learners' **line managers** or **mentors**
- the job performance of work-based learners as measured by the usual indicators
- other work-based indicators (eg rates of absence, spoilage, productivity) that can reasonably be attributed to specific training inputs
- any others peculiar to your particular situation.

And don't forget to consider *efficiency* also – ie how much professional **time, technology** and other resources has the project consumed? Might a redeployment of any of these resources have produced even more favourable outcomes?

If you are developing an MBL programme for external clients, try to ensure that appropriate indicators are used in evaluating the programme. Don't leave them to rely on their subjective impressions.

Evaluation—*get yourself a strategy*

Evaluation is any systematic attempt to find out what is going on in your MBL system, judge its acceptability and **effectiveness** and make any necessary decisions about it. In this book, I discuss its three chief forms under three headings: **commenting, developmental testing** and **monitoring**.

In training circles, and increasingly in education, lack of evaluation makes you vulnerable. If you can't demonstrate results (and **benefits**) you become an 'optional spend'. That is, your budget will be the first to be cut when times are hard. In my view, there are three main reasons for evaluating:

- *Political* – to convince people the teaching is effective, justify your use of resources and market your product.

- *Managerial* – to ensure the programme is running smoothly, people are working effectively and acceptable results are being attained. (See also **quality assurance**.)

- *Educational* – to aid **staff development** and **team**-building and, above all, to improve teaching and learning.

So, at an early stage of course planning (eg when developing a **course specification**), I suggest you prepare an evaluation *strategy* covering such questions as:

- What are the purposes of the evaluation – eg how might it help you manage, promote and improve the course?

- Who are the people most likely to be interested in or influenced by the outcomes of the evaluation?

- What aspects of the course need to be evaluated?

- What forms of effectiveness are we interested in?

- What kinds of data will need collecting?

- Who will collect the data?

- When and by what methods will it be collected?

- Who will interpret and report on the data?

- By when and to whom must reports be made?

- Who will help people interpret and take action on the basis of the reports?

- What political/ethical problems may arise?

- How much does the *budget* need to allow for evaluation?

Examinations—*MBL's necessary evil?*

Few words in the vocabulary of learning are more emotive than 'examinations'. Many people swear *by* them as the last bastion of civilization as we used to know it. Others (chiefly students) swear *at* them as sadistic instruments of torture. Throughout large tracts of education and training, exams have been all but replaced by coursework, continuous **assessment** and portfolios. Such methods are claimed to give more realistic assessment, enabling us to see how **learners** develop and offer them formative **feedback** – rather than waiting for a 'sudden death' occasion in rather artificial conditions that enables us to make a summative report on our learners but comes too late for them to learn from it.

So why might examinations still have a worthwhile role in MBL? Simply because the learners are likely to be less well known to their teachers than those in conventional learning. (Or less well known than such learners used to be before the recent worsening of learner-staff ratios.) Consequently, it may be necessary to ensure, at least from time to time, that the people producing the work for assessment purposes really are the ones who are enrolled for the course.

If there is no **accreditation** attached to your MBL, this may not matter much. You can give learners formative feedback on the assessment exercises they send you and if – as would be rather unlikely – they've had someone else do the work for them, well they're harming no one but themselves.

But if your course does carry some kind of degree, diploma or certificate in which you affirm the competence of the person named on it, then you need to guard against **cheating** (a frequent occurrence these days even in conventional teaching). Otherwise your MBL programme will be in danger of losing its **credibility**. So you may occasionally need to:

- give all learners a set task to perform at the same time
- make clear the precise nature of that task only when they are about to perform it (to avoid earlier collusion)
- have them perform it in the presence of an invigilator
- get the invigilator to check their passport photographs.

In short, you may need examinations – even if they are quite brief and infrequent and you give them no more weight than **assignments** and other coursework in deciding the learner's overall 'grade' for the course.

Existing materials—*not invented here?*

One sure way of wasting **time**, money and precious energy in MBL is to write your own **materials** when you don't need to. Many people massively under-estimate the time (and talent) needed to produce materials of the kind they associate with providers like the UK Open University and National Extension College. They (or their bosses) think, 'If you can teach, then you can write teaching materials – no problem.' In my experience, it can be rather a large problem, especially if you're having to carry on with your normal teaching load at the same time.

And yet thousands of learner-hours of effective material already exist. Look, for instance, at the bulging catalogues of the organizations mentioned above – or, if you're interested in vocational training, at the hundreds of **packages** listed in the annual *Open Learning Directory* published by Pergamon Press.

Maybe none of it will be relevant to your learners' needs. But do check it out first. Try not to dismiss usable material simply because it's not exactly how you would have written it. After all, you can always top and tail it with extra stuff of your own and provide alternative or supplementary material where you find deficiencies in the published product.

And don't feel you are restricted to using materials that were designed as 'open' or 'distance' learning packages. Consider also existing materials like published textbooks and articles or non-print resources like videos or computer software. These you might put together, again with whatever additional material you need to write yourself, and with your own **briefing** notes or 'wrap-around' **study guide** to talk your **learners** through the resource package you have assembled and engage them in appropriate learning **activities**.

Think also – if you and your learners have both the equipment and the necessary **study skills** – of the vast wealth of usable material (among a much more vast mass of rubbish) on the **Internet**. In addition, in UK universities, a librarian may be able to show you how to find resources through On-line Public Access Catalogues (OPACs).

There is no shame in using other people's materials – provided you can make them serve your learners' interests (and are careful about **copyright**). The less you need to write yourself, the more you can devote your energies to what can really make or break materials-based learning – that is, an effective learner **support** system.

Try not to reinvent too many wheels.

Face-to-face sessions—*let's meet*

This book is about materials-*based* learning, not about learning with **materials** alone. MBL does *not* exclude learning in company with other people.

Not all materials-based **learners** (especially those who have *chosen* to learn at a **distance**) will feel the need for face-to-face sessions with **tutors** or with other learners. But many will welcome the opportunity such sessions provide for **interactivity** and **feedback**. And you may decide that some such sessions are *essential* to the **integration** of your course design – both to ensure effective learning and to encourage the flow of supportive 'social **glue**'.

Below are just a few of the forms that such face-to-face sessions may take, depending on how easy it is to get your learners together. Remember that, even with those forms of MBL in which learners are all on the same site at the same time, they may have reached different points in the course.

- *Briefing or debriefing sessions* – in which the course leader sets the scene for the week's or month's MBL that lies ahead, sums up the work that has been done so far and maybe helps refresh learners' enthusiasm.

- *Occasional presentations* – in which visiting experts talk about some of the key themes of the course. (But they do not 'reteach' the **content** of the materials.)

- *Experience-sharing sessions* – in which learners share ideas and experience related to the MBL course. Especially relevant, perhaps, in professional development and in aesthetic or social areas – eg sales training, literary criticism, or child rearing.

- *Practical sessions* – where it is necessary for learners to do **practical work** under the guidance of an expert or to watch the experts show how it is done.

- *Remedial 'surgeries'* – for individuals or groups who are having occasional difficulties with the materials.

- *End-of-stage progress tests* – in which learners demonstrate what they have learned so far and are given feedback by a tutor, by a more experienced learner or by their **line manager** or a **mentor**.

So, would any such sessions be desirable (or even essential) for *your* materials-based learners? What problems might they raise for you or for your learners? What are the implications for **briefing** and **staff development**?

Failure—*some ways to make it happen*

This book is about how to make a success of MBL. All the same, it may be worth spending a page on some of the ways newcomers can go wrong. Here are just a few ways to *fail*:

✗ Impose MBL from the top down, commanding commitment from teachers, trainers, librarians, managers, etc – that is, from the only ones who can ensure it works properly.

✗ Alternatively, encourage individual enthusiasts to 'do their own thing' without **institutional support**.

✗ Don't waste **time** and resources on **consultation, briefing** people or **staff development**.

✗ Encourage the 'powers-that-be' in unrealistic expectations about likely cost-savings and about how quickly **materials** can be produced or new systems implemented.

✗ Assume that setting up an MBL course is basically a matter of repackaging one's existing **lecture** notes, etc.

✗ Expect staff to redesign their courses in their spare time and don't provide them with additional funding.

✗ **Reward** them for saving teaching time by giving them more people to teach; and don't take their MBL work into account in appraising them for tenure or promotion.

✗ Put most of your energies into developing materials or delivery **media** rather than into rethinking course design and learner **support** systems.

✗ Restrict yourself to a single teaching medium – eg printed workbooks or CD-ROMs or video-**conferencing**.

✗ Take it for granted that **learners** are well disposed towards MBL and already have the **study skills** to use it well.

✗ Specify rigidly what can and cannot be done in the name of MBL. (Don't allow local groups to develop variations geared to the needs of particular learners or contexts.)

✗ Set up ponderous decision-making systems (eg sluggish gate-keeping committees and inflexible **accounting** systems) that stifle new approaches.

✗ Make brave changes in two or three aspects of your system but don't ask whether they might be scuppered by changes that have *not* been made elsewhere in the system.

✗ Ignore other organizations' experience with MBL unless it suits your hopes and beliefs. (In which case, assume that what was true for them will also be true for you.)

Feedback—*and how to make it flow*

Feedback is the key to **quality** in education and training. Unless **learners** get feedback from us, they won't be sure how well they are learning. (And unless we get feedback from them, we won't know how well we are teaching.) Feedback is what enables us *all* to learn from our experience.

Unfortunately, feedback needs regular contact with other people – eg with **tutors** or at least other learners. By definition, however, that's exactly what MBL learners have less of than most – unless someone builds it into the system.

Some kinds of learning **material** claim to have feedback built into them (along with **activities**). But learners need more than these specimen answers or comment paragraphs, which say the same thing to every reader of the material. They need more even than the kind of computer-based **interactivity** that enables them to tap in some input and get an instant pre-programmed response (helpful though that may be).

What learners need is something *personal* – a response from another human being who has understood how things seem to them and is able to say something that challenges or confirms their understanding, and helps them overcome errors or encourages them towards new insights. (See also **individualization**.)

Personal feedback (of different kinds) may be provided by:

- tutors or trainers (eg in learning **centres** or at a **distance**)
- librarians or technicians in learning centres
- **mentors** or **line managers**
- other learners, or their family and friends.

This feedback may be given:

- in **face-to-face sessions** – eg by tutors or trainers, line managers, mentors, or other learners in **self-help groups**.
- in writing – eg by tutors commenting on learners' **assignments** or **examination** scripts or by tutors and other learners taking part in **conferencing**.
- on the telephone – eg by tutors at the end of a **help line**.

Finally, don't forget that we too – the course providers – need feedback. We need it to help us identify deficiencies in our materials or **support** system and improve them where we can. That's why we need **commenting, developmental testing, evaluation, monitoring** and **quality assurance**.

Feelings—*dealing with the irrational*

When working with people in MBL, especially if they are new to it, you may be surprised to find that they sometimes:

- don't mean what they say

- don't say what they mean

- don't do what they say

- don't know what they mean

- don't know the meaning of what they say or do.

That is so in any area of social activity, you may say. True, but it may strike you more forcibly with MBL because the people involved showed no such tendencies before they became involved with MBL!

Compared with 'conventional' teaching and training, new participants may find there are quite a few things to be anxious about. And their concerns may not be ones they care to admit to or discuss too openly. Such undisclosed fears and desires may result in puzzling and disruptive behaviour.

Moving into MBL makes teachers and trainers rather vulnerable and liable to **stress**. They are probably being expected to learn new ways of doing things (and probably of seeing things) at great speed while at the same time keeping up the momentum of their original system. Some may wonder whether they really can learn the new ways, eg of developing **materials** or of coaching **learners** at a **distance** (especially if new **technology** is involved). Others may find the new experience of working in **teams** is nerve-racking – especially when their output benefits from **commenting** (however constructive) by colleagues. Some will be struggling to keep out of trouble, others to carve out new empires for themselves. A few may be angry or resentful about other members in the team. Many will fear for their jobs. Not everyone will be pursuing the official **aims** of the group.

I'm not saying that every MBL system should provide a relationships counsellor for its staff, though I've heard of some that do. But don't be surprised if colleagues sometimes behave in seemingly irrational ways. Maybe this indicates some feeling that they have not seen fit to share with you. Who knows? Perhaps you have some such feelings yourself? If we feel safe, maybe we can discuss some of our less productive feelings. Perhaps together we can then consider their origins and even do something to overcome them.

Flexibilities—*how far can you bend?*

Developing MBL courses? Just a matter of revamping our old **lecture** notes, right? Wrong. Apart from the vital need for **support** as well as **materials**, effective materials-based learning may well suggest, or even demand, that you rethink and *redesign* your course.

In particular, you may see the need or the opportunity to improve **access** and **user-friendliness**, to allow for **diversity** among your **learners** and their **milieux** and to provide for more **individualization**. You may need to make your course more flexible. You may want to do this in any of a variety of ways – eg by enabling learners to:

- start the course whenever they wish (or at least more often than once a year)

- negotiate their own completion times (for the course as a whole and the sections within it)

- get exemption from parts of the course (and thus save time and money) because of their prior learning (**APL**).

- learn when and where they please

- decide their own sequence through the sections of the course

- exercise some control over the **objectives** and **content** of the course (eg by choosing among sections or by **projects**)

- relate the course to their professional or social lives (eg through work-based or community-based **assignments**)

- have the course 'versioned' to suit the needs of learners wanting to work on it as a group (eg in an organization or a community group)

- have some choice of **media**, eg texts or multimedia, computer **conferencing** or **face-to-face sessions**

- choose who they will get help from, eg **tutors**, **mentors**, librarians, **line managers**, **self-help groups**, etc

- have a choice of **assessment** methods and types of **accreditation** – eg written exercises vs workplace competence tests; degrees vs vocational qualifications

- build on the course to reach higher level, eg from certificate to diploma to degree.

Which forms of flexibility might you need to build into *your* MBL courses if you are to attract and keep the learners you are hoping to serve?

Glue—*the kind that holds people together*

Much MBL can be rather impersonal. There may be dozens, hundreds or even thousands of **learners** on any given course. We'll give them plenty of learning **materials** to keep them busy. Yet our learners may never meet each other. They may be far apart geographically, or they may be learning in much the same place but at different times. Each may feel they are on their own – alone in a scattered crowd.

Such learners miss out on the feeling of being part of a group, moving through a shared experience with common purpose. They have no one with whom to discuss a problem and cut it down to size; no one with whom to compare themselves or swap stimulus; no one with whom to chew the fat and have a few sustaining laughs. As a result, they can suffer **stress**, lose their **motivation**, get alienated – and become **drop-outs**.

What such learners are missing is what my colleague Graham Gibbs calls 'social glue' – something in addition to the materials that binds them to the course and to one another. (Incidentally, when MBL *staff* are working at a **distance** from one another, they too may become unglued.)

How might you spread some glue in *your* system? Maybe you can get people together 'in the flesh' more often, eg:

- group induction (and socializing) sessions for all learners (and for **support** staff) as they start the course
- periodic **face-to-face sessions** of a kind that get learners relating to one another rather than simply to the course
- **projects** that require learners to collaborate in groups
- residential sessions at weekends or in holidays
- **self-help groups**
- social gatherings (eg for sports, travel or theatre visits) which may or may not be course-related
- updating and experience-sharing **workshops** for staff.

Failing this, or as a supplement, you may be able to create a 'virtual' glue-spreading **milieu** – for example, through:

- **newsletters**, enabling learners both to hear what other people are up to and send in their own contributions
- computer **conferencing**, especially of a kind that gets learners collaborating in groups
- audio- or video-conferencing, with learners responding to one another rather than to the 'sage on the stage'.

Gradualism—*one step at a time*

In the cheering words of Lao-Tsu: 'A journey of a thousand miles must begin with a single step.' Worth remembering if you're impressed by the potential **benefits** of MBL but feel daunted at the task of getting a system up and running. Maybe there's only you, and maybe you've got little in the way of resources and nothing at all in the way of **institutional support**.

So how might you set about turning a **lecture**-based course into MBL? Gradually, that's how. Work step by step. Don't try to transform all your course at once, but keep building on what you have learned so far. Be ready to take two or three years to reach the level of MBL you feel comfortable with.

There are many different first steps you could take (maybe have already taken). Here are a few that occur to me.

- Provide **learners** with a **course guide**.

- Give them a reading list with your detailed notes about what to look out for and what to ignore in each item.

- Set them **activities, assignments** or group **projects** based on one of the items.

- Replace certain lectures with a **study guide** consisting of your lecture notes (tidied up) plus activities or problems to be tackled and brought to the next **face-to-face session**.

- Photocopy a set of readings for a part of your course (if you or your students can afford the **copyright** and print costs).

- Produce an audio-tape with printed study guide (or a video-tape if your topic needs moving pictures) to replace **lectures** or demonstrations in part of your course.

- Gather together sets of books, articles and non-print resources focused on separate course topics, split your class into groups and get them to work on each set in turn.

- Get learners using MBL material from elsewhere (eg the Open University) as one week's work on the course.

- Reduce the frequency of group face-to-face sessions and introduce **help lines** and regular 'surgeries'.

- Develop **assessment** methods that encourage learners to work in **self-help groups** and aid one another's learning.

- Swap materials with a colleague in another department or organization – or agree to develop some in **collaboration**.

- Bid for **time** and funds to build on the proven **effectiveness** you have achieved so far on a shoestring!

Help lines—*supporting at a distance*

Materials-based **learners** tend to spend a lot of time working on their own or in small, isolated groups. Either way, they can't easily buttonhole a **tutor** informally and try an idea out on them or get help or reassurance with some problem they're being flummoxed by. If this is likely to be so in your MBL system, you may want to consider setting up a help line – some means whereby learners can get a fairly rapid response. Without it, many learners might quickly despair, lose **motivation** and become **drop-outs** – all for want of what might be simply a few timely words from a tutor or **mentor**.

Incidentally, if you are working with a **team** of colleagues, some of whom rarely meet each other – eg tutors located at some **distance** from one another and central staff – they too might welcome a help line connection to someone who can give instant decisions or advice.

This most basic form of **support** has traditionally been provided by telephone. In my experience, learners who use it are usually very appreciative; but many who might benefit are reluctant to 'bother' the tutor. To overcome such reluctance, tutors often need to be very specific about the times when they will be available and probably need to make the first few contacts themselves. They may also need to develop strategies for dealing with learners who require or expect more time than the circumstances can reasonably allow. (What **staff development** might such tutors need?)

Both the reluctance to presume on the tutor's time and the opposite tendency to occupy them for a whole evening can, to an extent, be overcome by replacing telephones with some of the newer **media**. Help lines based on fax and e-mail may be seen by reluctant learners as less intrusive on the tutor's time and tutors can deal with the more demanding learners at a time and extent of their own choice. And if tutors and learners are in touch via computer **conferencing,** then a learner's cry for help may be answered by other learners before the tutor has even noticed it. Such media also allow the cry to go out at any time of day or night.

If you have **Internet** access and you'd like to join (free) a US-based but international online discussion group for people wanting to share ideas about applying **technology** to advising learners, try sending the message 'Subscribe TECADV-L (your name)' to 'LISTSERV@UAFSYSB.UARK.EDU'.

Images of learning—*do they match?*

Your **learners** may not view learning in the same way as you do. Indeed, they may show **diversity** among themselves. What frustrations and misunderstandings might arise if you and your colleagues were working with one of the following four images in mind and your learners with *different* ones?

1 *Learning as memorizing.* Learners (and teachers?) who hold this most basic conception of learning will be concerned largely with rote learning of facts and procedures that can be reproduced under test conditions. This is the 'Mastermind' or 'University Challenge' image of learning.

2 *Learning as understanding.* Learners holding this more sophisticated image will not be satisfied simply to recall and reproduce the facts and procedures they've been working with. They will search for ways to make them meaningful – perhaps looking for the ideas that lie behind them, or the patterns, trends and relationships that help make sense of it all, or the links with their own beliefs and values.

3 *Learning as application.* Learners who've reached the third conception will go further still. They will expect to apply their new understanding in some context they are concerned about – and in the process perhaps develop new ideas and procedures of their own. They expect their learning to help them see the world differently and perhaps find new ways of making things happen in it.

4 *Learning as personal development.* In this most sophisticated conception, learners recognize that they themselves are part of the world they might come to see or act upon differently. The learner expects to be changed as a person by the experience of learning. Even when the detail is forgotten, that experience will have left them, in some sense, a wiser and more capable person.

Learners may see learning differently from their teachers or trainers. And this could present a barrier to learning. If, for example, the **assessment** system is operating with image 2 or 3 when your learners are concerned with image 1 or 4, frustration looms. So it may be worth asking your learners what they think of as learning, and helping them to see how their image relates to what your programme might be expecting of them. It may even be one of the **aims** of your programme to help them acquire more sophisticated images of learning. And is it worth checking that you and your *colleagues* have compatible **images of teaching**?

Images of teaching—*which is yours?*

Just as **learners** have their different **images of learning,** teachers and trainers have their own different views of what *teaching* is all about. For example, do you see it chiefly as a matter of conveying an accepted body of knowledge to your learners which they must take on board and be able to reproduce? Or are you more interested in enabling your learners to play a part themselves in the construction of their knowledge? How would you feel about asking your learners questions you don't know the answers to? Do you see yourself as doing things *to* the learners or *with* them? Are your learners empty vessels to be filled or flames to be lit?

That last sentence reminds us that teachers and trainers often talk about their work using analogies or metaphors. Here are four I have often noticed:

Medical. The teacher or trainer sees it as his or her job to diagnose some deficit or weaknesses in the learner and then prescribe and apply a treatment that will lead to an improvement in the learner's educational health.

House-building. The teacher's job is to take the 'bricks and mortar' of existing knowledge and, following a detailed plan, reassemble an identical edifice or structure in all learners' minds – a structure they will not be able to 'occupy' and make effective use of until it is completed.

Gardening. The teacher may have a broad plan as to what he or she will grow in the learners' minds but realizes that the 'ground' itself (the learners) will influence what grows best in each 'garden' and that no two will be the same – and none the worse for that.

Voyaging. A diverse group embark together on a journey or expedition, each perhaps bringing different hopes and skills but one of them (the teacher), being a more experienced voyager, is the natural leader and navigator. Even if the group sets off towards a firm destination, each may make something different of it when they arrive and gain different insights and pleasures from the voyage itself.

You and your colleagues may suggest yet other analogies or metaphors. How closely do you all agree? How compatible are your views with your learners' **motivations** and images of learning? You may want to share your ideas when planning the **aims** and **objectives** of your MBL. Conflicting images of teaching could lead to inappropriate learning **activities** and **assessment** – thus lessening the **effectiveness** of your course.

Individualization—*what about me?*

Much MBL can be rather impersonal. To be sure, the learning **materials** may be written with great care but they are not directed at anyone in particular. Every **learner** on the course may get presented with exactly the same **content**, in exactly the same **media**, in exactly the same sequence.

This recorded teaching makes no attempt, as a live human teacher might, to adapt itself to the interests and concerns of an individual learner. The recorded teaching does not ask about the learner's experiences or problems, let alone use those experiences and problems as a focus for the teaching.

As a result, the learner may be alienated. That is, he or she may feel separate from the learning. Most learners will benefit from having someone who can react to them as *individuals* – someone who can respond to each learner's personal needs and concerns. For example, by:

- providing **entry** (and exit) **counselling** to learners and helping them select appropriate learning materials

- adapting learning materials to suit the needs of an individual learner

- agreeing a plan of **support** with individual learners, assessing their progress at intervals and giving them helpful **feedback**.

- offering individuals general guidance about **study skills** and help with specific learning difficulties

- commenting on learners' responses to exercises, **activities**, **assignments**, etc

- coaching or counselling learners, individually, via a **help-line** or **face-to-face**, and running group sessions

- helping learners get support from other people, eg a **line manager** at their workplace

- assessing learners' knowledge, understanding and practical competence

- guiding learners in pursuit of understanding through their own chosen topics, eg in individual **projects**

- helping learners apply their new learning to their jobs.

Who will provide *your* learners with this kind of individual support? What kind of **institutional support** might those *supporters* need? And how will it be provided?

Institutional support—*top-down help*

Most teaching and training organizations are now under pressure to do more with less. More students or trainees, less per head to spend on them. This often means finding new methods of dealing with them – often methods involving MBL. This in turn means new pressures on staff to change their ways and develop new skills and values. Can they do it? Will they want to? This largely depends on the amount and kind of support that MBL gets from senior management.

For instance, has your institution:

- made a public statement of its intentions and **quality assurance** standards for the use of MBL?

- rethought its use of space (eg teaching spaces, learning **centres**, library, workshops etc) to facilitate a shift to MBL?

- encouraged staff involvement by measuring their output in terms of how many hours of learning they support rather than how many hours they teach?

- released staff from other teaching duties to give them time to rethink their courses and develop **materials**?

- devolved budgets and provided accurate information about costs to groups and project **teams** so that they can make their own realistic decisions in **costing MBL**?

- minimized any obstruction from committees controlling resources or likely to delay decision-making?

- shifted funding from delivery to development costs and shown itself willing to provide up-front investment?

- provided printing and other **production** facilities enabling staff to produce multiple copies of materials with minimum fuss and expense?

- set up a **record-keeping** system that can keep track of **learner** progress and trigger staff action where needed?

- thought out and resourced a strategy for **staff development** and sharing of experience about MBL?

- made teaching excellence an explicit and high-priority criterion for the promotion of staff?

- ensured that staff who develop innovative teaching can expect the **rewards** to outweigh the hassle?

Many organizations are good at willing the ends but not all are so good at willing the means. Policy statements come cheap; making them work is rather more costly.

Integration—*fitting each to its own*

At a recent materials-planning **workshop** of mine, one of the participants was thinking about what her computer-based **learners** would need to do in **face-to-face sessions** before and after the materials-based work and which of those **materials** she should be giving them in print rather than on the screen. She wanted the various components of her teaching/learning system to be properly integrated – with each of her **media** used because it was most fit for its purpose.

There are many 'single solution' merchants around in MBL. These are enthusiasts who talk as though one medium (eg printed workbooks, CD-ROM, video **conferencing**) will solve all your educational problems. But this is not so. Different media have their different strengths and weaknesses. Our challenge is to choose the mixture of media that best suits our learners' needs and course **objectives** and *combine* them so that each medium does what it can do best, and only that.

Furthermore, this book is about materials-*based* learning, *not* about learning that relies solely on materials. Materials may be all your learners need for certain subjects, especially when they are dealing with concepts and principles and even with the ideas behind procedures and **practical** skills. But, when it comes to *practising* those procedures and practical skills – especially if they involve relating to other people – they may need to get **feedback** from **support** staff or other learners. So you may need to integrate face-to-face sessions of some kind with the learners' work on their materials. Even if face-to-face sessions are not made essential by the course objectives, they may still be desirable – to motivate and cheer up your learners, and to spread the 'social **glue**'.

Until recently, materials-based learning almost always implied distance learning – though most successful distance teaching integrated its distance media with 'conventional' features like tutorials and summer schools. But, in recent years, 'distance learning' has come on site. Learners may be working on print-based or computer-driven packages as *part* of a largely conventional course. Or some of their courses may be mainly materials-based and others mainly class-based.

So the question to ask is *not*: 'Shall we replace conventional courses with materials-based learning?' Rather it is: 'Given *these* particular learners and *these* particular learning needs, which aspects of the course shall learners tackle by working alone on materials and which by individual or class contact with teachers or trainers and with other learners?'

Interactivity—*getting a response*

Part of the buzz of classroom learning comes from making things happen. **Learners** can talk to one another and get a response. They can question their teacher or trainer and try to get a satisfying answer. They can practise new ideas or skills on one another and see what happens. They are not learning passively. Nor are they active merely in learning an inert body of knowledge. The situation is *inter*active. What they do can *change* what they are learning. They are shaping the subject between them and making it their own.

Many materials-based learners – especially those learning at a **distance** – are denied much of this. Learning **materials** (like many **lectures**) have usually been a one-way street, conveying **content** from the notebooks of the teachers or trainers into the notebooks of the learners. They have had no mechanism for getting the learners' ideas into play. Learners couldn't say: 'What do you mean by that?' or 'How would this experience of mine fit in with what you are saying?' To get a response from somebody they would need to go outside the materials and look to **self help groups, face-to-face sessions, correspondence teaching, help lines** and the like.

One of the advantages of new **technology** is that it can make learning more interactive. With CD-ROM and multimedia learners can enjoy the satisfactions (and often confusions) of working out their own individual route around a **package**, following their own interests and perhaps seeing materials that other learners do not see. 'Simulation' packages (in which, for example, the learner may be experimenting with a nuclear reactor or a hospital patient) go further. They can be interactive in the same way as a computer game – with the learner being able to try things out (eg on the reactor or the patient) and see what happens next.

Paradoxically, however, the new technology also enables interactivity (and **individualization**) of the human kind. The **conferencing** media, and especially computer conferencing, enable teachers or trainers and learners to give each other **feedback**, either in speech or writing, of the sorts I described in the first paragraph above. They can try things out on one another and get a fairly rapid response from other people.

How far will the success of *your* MBL system depend on your learners being able to get the teaching to respond to them? To what extent will it be necessary for this response to come from people (rather than from pre-programmed software)? How might you arrange for such interactivity?

Internet—*finding materials world-wide*

Despite the irritating hype, the Internet has a lot to offer the materials-based **learner** – too much, in some respects. Provided your learner has access to a suitably connected computer, she or he can call up (and print off) **materials** held on millions of computers around the world. (You may be interested to visit some of the sample sites listed on page 124.)

Material is available in three main forms:

E-mail. Your learners will be able to send material from their computers to those of their **tutors** or other learners anywhere in the world. Besides text messages they may be able to send spreadsheets, databases, software and (though not very conveniently yet) audio and video files.

One off-shoot of e-mail, computer **conferencing**, enables tutors and learners to send messages to the whole group at once (or to sub-groups), enabling peer teaching and collaborative small-group work.

Discussion groups. There are thousands of different discussion groups covering practically every imaginable topic of interest to humanity, including, surely, every subject that might concern teachers and trainers. These groups (or 'lists') act like a public notice-board on which people can leave messages and read other people's. Your learner sends a comment (or responds to one) to, say, the 'chem-tech' or 'law-europe' list and everyone who also follows that list will see it and some may amplify or challenge it, setting off a discussion. (See page 124.)

World Wide Web. Universities, colleges, libraries, training organizations and commercial companies, government departments, newspapers and journals around the world have made available (free) a wealth of material to anyone who gets her or his computer to contact theirs. This material includes articles, photographs, audio and video materials, software and information of all conceivable kinds . Many items offer direct links (at the click of one's 'mouse') to related information on yet other computers.

However, information is not knowledge and knowledge is certainly not wisdom. Making information easily available is therefore not the same as teaching and does not necessarily result in worthwhile learning. If learners are to gain wisdom from this tempting but potentially overwhelming resource, what new **study skills** might they need to develop? And what other forms of **structure** and **support** might they need from your **learning system** to help them learn effectively?

Job descriptions—*who's to do what?*

MBL schemes sometimes go adrift because certain key tasks get neglected, eg providing **commenting** on colleagues' material or **support** to work-based **learners**. And the reason they are neglected may be that they have never been made clear to the people concerned. They simply didn't realize they were meant to be doing them.

On the other hand, people sometimes assume they are meant to carry out certain tasks when they aren't. This can lead to them stepping on other people's toes when they do try to carry them out and turning sulky when asked to desist.

When appointing **consultants** and staff who will work with us on a limited project, we may be careful to give them a **contract** that spells out just what they are agreeing to do. When appointing **team** members from existing staff, however, we may easily overlook the need for such clarity. But we can't assume that they know exactly what they are letting themselves in for by joining our team. What do they know of the many **roles** that may need to be carried out and which we have in mind for them? In particular, do they know if we are expecting them to carry out more than one? This may not be obvious from their current job descriptions.

Lack of an appropriate job description (or any at all) can make it difficult if you need, for example, to remonstrate with a hard-pressed course author about why they aren't providing comments on their colleague's **materials** or to placate a **tutor** about why they aren't being paid to help write any of the course materials. They can justifiably say: 'Nobody told me' or 'I thought I could take it for granted.'

Similarly, if you are providing MBL for work-based learners, what role is expected of their **line manager**? The learners' success may depend very much on the quality of support they get from their line manager. But the manager, whose prime concerns will be operational, may well say: 'Why should I be expected to help them learn? Training is the training department's job. It's not in my job description.'

Do you see potential problems here in your MBL system? How relevant is your own job description? Perhaps we should review one another's job descriptions at the start of any new project and amend them if new tasks are to be expected of us. This may make it more likely that all relevant aspects of our performance will be discussed at **appraisal** time and help us argue the case for appropriate **rewards**.

Learners—*what's crucial about yours?*

Who are your learners? What do you know about them? The more you know or can find out, the better you'll be able to focus your **materials** and your **support** system. (See also **anticipation**.) For example:

Demographic factors

- How many learners are you likely to have?
- How old are they?
- What sex and race?
- Any with personal disabilities?
- Occupations (if any)?
- Where in the site/country/world will they be learning?

Motivation

- Why are they learning?
- How might your programme relate to their lives or work?
- What do they want from the programme?
- What are their hopes and fears?

Learning factors

- What **images** do they hold about learning?
- What **learning styles** do they prefer?
- What **study skills** do they have?
- What experience of, and **attitudes** to, MBL?

Subject background

- How do they feel about the subject of the programme?
- What related knowledge/skills do they already have?
- What misconceptions or inappropriate habits?
- What relevant personal interests and experience?

Resource factors

- Where, when and how will they be learning?
- Who will be paying their costs?
- How much time will they have available?
- What access will they have to **media**/facilities?
- What access to human support – eg **tutors** or **mentors**?

You don't know? Then ask them! (See **market research**.)

Learning styles—*catering for diversity*

What do you know about your **learners'** learning styles? How different are they? How far can you cater for different styles in your **materials** and in your **support** system?

Learning styles have been categorized in many different ways, eg serialist vs holist, convergent vs divergent, surface level vs deep level, and verbalising vs imaging. Some learners may use one style for all learning tasks; some may switch styles according to the varying demands our programmes are making on them. (See Schmeck, 1988.)

Honey and Mumford (1986), for example, distinguish between Activists, Theorists, Pragmatists or Reflectors. They give detailed guidance about the kinds of learning **activities** that someone is likely to respond to well or poorly if they prefer one or other of these learning styles. For instance:

STYLES	respond WELL to, eg	respond POORLY to, eg
Activists *'Here, let me do that.'*	New problems, being thrown in at the deep end, team work. . .	Passive learning, solitary work, theory, precise instructions. . .
Theorists *'Yes, but how do you justify it?'*	Interesting concepts, structured situations, opportunities to question and probe. . .	Lack of apparent context or purpose, ambiguity and uncertainty, doubts about validity. . .
Pragmatists *'So long as it works.'*	Relevance to real problems, immediate chance to try things out, experts they can emulate. . .	Abstract theory, lack of practice or clear guidelines, no obvious benefit from learning. . .
Reflectors *'I need time to consider that.'*	Thinking things through, painstaking research, detached observation. . .	Being forced into the limelight, acting without planning, time pressures. . .

No MBL programme can be right for everyone all the time. But it's useful to remember the **diversity** of learning styles. Not everyone learns like you do. So try to ensure everyone gets a fair chance to do things their way at least some of the time. Otherwise, prepare to start counting your **drop-outs**.

You may also plan to help your learners acquire *new* learning styles. To do so may make them more flexible and effective.

Learning systems—*your added value*

There's a lot more to materials-based learning than **materials**. Anyone can churn out materials from which people can learn. Publishers do it. Broadcasters do it. Computer software producers do it. And, since the dawn of **Internet**, the very ether seems to be teeming with potential learning resources.

But there's a big difference between 'delivering information' and providing a *learning system*. Without the system, learning may be painful, misdirected and ineffective. So what else, besides materials, might you need to provide?

- *Publicity*. How will you bring the learning opportunity to the attention of people who might benefit from **access**?

- *Enrolment*. How will you control entry, eg by fees, **prerequisites**, or self-selection? Will you help potential **learners** with **entry counselling**?

- *Contracts*. Learners and 'providers' need to agree as to what they can expect or demand from one another.

- *Structure*. Most learners need **objectives** to aim at, well-sequenced **activities** that will get them there and **deadlines** they're expected to meet along the way.

- *Resources*. Not just learning materials but maybe also learning **centres**, transport, help with expenses, and so on.

- *Personal help*. What if learners have difficulty with the materials or need **feedback** about how they are doing? The system needs to include people they can rely on for personal **support** – usually **tutors** or **mentors**.

- *Care*. Learners benefit from knowing that someone cares about their individual welfare and progress in learning.

- *Community support*. Ideally, the system should foster a learning **milieu** in which learners feel part of a community that shares goals and experience and offers mutual support.

- *Records*. If learners are to get appropriate support and **accreditation**, sensitive **record-keeping** is essential.

- *Accreditation*. The system needs to ensure that learners can demonstrate what they have achieved and obtain the qualifications that certify to their achievement.

- *Quality*. What **quality assurance** is undertaken to ensure that learners and their sponsors (if any) are receiving the products and services they are entitled to expect?

So what will *your* system need to provide, besides materials?

Lectures—*and other passive teaching*

Lectures are the very essence of what most people think of as 'conventional' courses. They are becoming more so (and the audiences are getting bigger) as staff/learner ratios worsen. Some teachers and trainers like them – they enable you to deliver your **content** with what seems like a minimum of fuss. But they've long had a bad press with many **learners** and education experts – largely because they demand too much passive listening (far beyond most people's normal concentration span) and provide little opportunity for **interactivity** (eg swapping questions and answers between lecturer and learners, or learners and learners) – with the result that most of the lecturer's content goes to waste.

But why mention lectures in a book about materials-based learning? For two reasons.

Firstly, even if your learners are working entirely at a **distance**, they may still encounter passive, lecture-type teaching among their **materials** (or their **conferencing**). How so? Because many distance teachers are content-driven. Their texts or videos or whatever they say to learners are pretty much what they would be saying if they had a hall full of people in front of them. They haven't taken account of the fact that people learn by doing. Effective MBL is built around **activities** that get the learner applying the content. Otherwise, faced with a stream of content unbroken by any invitation to use it, learners are only too likely to assume that their task must be to memorize as much as possible.

Secondly, your MBL course may include some **face-to-face sessions**. If so, is there a risk that these could degenerate into a string of lectures? Some **tutors** may feel happier about holding forth than about struggling to get to grips with learners' idiosyncratic perceptions of the subject matter. Many learners may also want lectures, preferring to be talked at and perhaps saved the trouble of working too hard with the course materials. (The tutors who hold regular group sessions in the Inland Revenue's MBL scheme have been expressly forbidden to reteach the content of the materials.)

You may feel occasional lectures (or lecture-type materials) are acceptable – provided they are short, stimulating and lead on to activities. But face-to-face sessions are surely too precious to waste on delivering information – not when we could be using the time on what cannot so easily be done at a distance – eg small-group work, **individualization**, **practical work** and problem-solving, and spreading the 'social **glue**'.

Libraries—*places, people and resources*

Libraries have always been important to people who are learning on their own. They still can be. But their potential is misunderstood and not used as well as it might be.

Distance learners, for example, may find it difficult to get to a library at all. Even if they can, their library may not be able to provide them with the perhaps rather specialist material you want them to study.

What about work-based or on-campus **learners**? All educational campuses will have a library. So will many employers. But will such libraries have what materials-based learners need? Whether in workplaces or campuses, libraries are usually more geared to supporting individual specialists rather than dozens (or hundreds) of learners all seeking the same basic books or journal articles at the same time.

In further and higher education, libraries have been kept short of cash for the last ten years or more. At the same time, book and journal prices have doubled or trebled, far more than the general rise in inflation. Hence, libraries have been less and less able to hold multiple copies of basic texts – which learners are increasingly not buying for themselves because they can't afford them either.

We can take some of the pressure off libraries by redesigning our courses so that not all our learners need the same books at the same time (see **gradualism**). Increased use of computer **conferencing**, CD-ROM databases and the **Internet** may also open up new possibilities, but at a cost. And where multiple copies of course **materials** are needed, we may need to provide them out of non-library budgets and/or require learners to buy them from us at cost.

Libraries will still be a valuable source of material for more specialist learning, eg for individual **project** work. And they may also provide a congenial place to study (see **centres**) – though on-campus learners may find the seating rather limited since the recent explosion in student numbers.

Remember also that librarians, as professional information-handlers, can play a vital role in developing and supporting MBL. They can help teachers and trainers seek out and evaluate research sources and **existing materials** for learning. They can also be in the front line of helping learners learn. Indeed, many public libraries in the UK are now offering an 'open learning service' which entails both providing learning **packages** and equipment and helping learners get **support**.

Line managers—*for workplace support*

Do your **learners** need or wish to apply what they are learning to their work? If so, the role of their line manager can be crucial. It may, in fact, be their boss who has suggested (or demanded) they do the learning in the first place. In which case, we might hope that he or she will provide appropriate help and resources while they get on with it.

Some line managers see training and **staff development** as the responsibility of a training or personnel department. They may even regard training as a nuisance – disruptive to production or the smooth running of their department. Yet others may simply be unaware that a member of their staff is doing an MBL course that might be relevant to their job.

The **attitudes** of line managers can make or break MBL in a vocational context – especially if staff are reluctant learners to start with. Where line managers think the programme is disruptive they certainly won't support, and may well discourage, the learners. ('You don't want to bother with that stuff; I didn't need it to get where I am today.' Or simply 'Do it if you want – so long as it's in your own time.')

But well-disposed line managers can help in many ways, eg:

- discussing new ideas/procedures introduced in the course
- talking over any problems and difficulties that arise
- helping learners relate their learning to their work
- contributing to work-based learning **activities**
- discussing **assignments** the learner will submit to a **tutor**
- helping review the **feedback** from tutor
- providing access to resources not normally available
- allowing the learner time for study at the workplace
- assessing learners' workplace competence, eg for Scottish or National Vocational Qualifications (in the UK).

So how might you help line managers become 'well-disposed', and ensure they have appropriate knowledge and skills? At very least this calls for **consultation** and **briefing**. If their contribution is to be extensive, **staff development** may be needed, not to mention provision of suitable **rewards**, an alteration to their **job description** and relevant discussion at **appraisal** time. It may also pay to encourage them in the use of MBL for their own career development (eg an MBA) thus turning them into **alumni** and possibly **champions** of MBL.

Managing MBL—*what's involved?*

Managing MBL can be more complex than managing
'conventional' learning – especially if it involves course
production as well as presentation. As with managing any
activity, there are four key tasks:

* Plan what needs doing (activities and goals).
* Organize the right people to do it.
* Monitor what they do.
* Make any corrections needed to keep to your goals.

Here are some of the main things that may need doing – in
roughly the order they are likely to *begin* being important:

1 Carry out **market research**.
2 Consult colleagues and seek **champions** in the organization
  or elsewhere.
3 Develop **course specifications**.
4 Estimate **costing** and obtain financing.
5 Select or recruit and **brief** or train suitable staff.
6 Develop **quality** standards.
7 Find or develop suitable **materials**.
8 Develop **assessment** system.
9 Set up learner **support** system.
10 Set up **record-keeping** system.
11 Market course and recruit **learners**.
12 Foster the most conducive possible learning **milieu**.
13 Monitor activities and take any needed corrective action.
14 Evaluate the course and improve it where possible.
15 Reflect on the experience of 1–14 and learn from it.

Perhaps you can see additional activities that will need
managing in your context? And, of course, each of the activities
I have listed could be broken down into more specific tasks. You
will find more details about many of them throughout this
book. The bold type above may suggest where to start looking,
but also try: **consultation, evaluation, monitoring, staff
development** and whatever other topics seem relevant to you
(especially under the heading 'Setting up and managing an
MBL programme or system') on page 6.

Market research—*what will they buy?*

What might you and your colleagues be able to offer that other people might be willing to pay for? This is a new question for most teachers and trainers. But it needs to be explored before you incur too many costs in developing a new course. Unless you can run it at a loss, you'll need to be sure first (and probably convince others) that either:

1 enough **learners** will be willing to pay the fees that you'll need to charge, or

2 their sponsors will be willing to contribute to the development or running costs. (See **costing MBL**.)

We are no longer safe in putting on just whatever courses we want to put on, secure in knowing that they will attract plenty of learners. If we don't make a serious attempt to find out what our likely **'customers'** want (and offer it) we simply won't get enough learners to enable us to stay in work.

More and more of our potential learners (and such sponsors as employers or government agencies) are expecting us to respond to their individual **needs**. Hence the many new approaches like competence-based **assessment**, workplace-related **assignments**, **accreditation** of prior learning (**APL**), modular courses and, especially, the huge increase in part-time, **distance** learning.

So will you and your colleagues be able to provide something that learners (or their sponsors) might be willing to pay for? Here are six suggestions for some basic market research.

* Keep aware of what competing organizations are providing and not providing.

* Analyse **feedback** (including complaints) from present learners and sponsors about your existing courses.

* Draft possible new programmes for discussion with them.

* Consult widely, eg – learners on your present courses; **alumni**; sponsors of present or past learners; potential sponsors; people in your organization; people outside.

* Gather information (and set up a database) eg by reading; postal surveys via questionnaires; interviews and focus groups; discussions via e-mail and **Internet**.

* Aim to build up a picture of how many learners there might be, who might sponsor them, what they will be willing to pay, what they might want from and bring to a course, what problems they might have – and what you might be able to offer that your competitors cannot.

Materials—*seven main options*

Clearly, in a materials-based learning system, materials are of the essence. **Learners** may use **existing materials**, some perhaps not developed with learners in mind, eg books, journals, newspapers, videos, **Internet** resources. Or they may use specially compiled learning **packages.**

A learning system may deploy such materials in at least seven different ways.

1 'Here is the syllabus; the **examination** will be a year from now; see you then' (In other words, 'Decide what learning materials you might find suitable – and buy, borrow, beg or steal them wherever you can.')

2 'As in 1, but *past examination papers (and examiners' reports) will be made available on request.'* (As before, 'Decide what learning materials you might find suitable – and buy, borrow, beg or steal them wherever you can.')

3 'As in 2, but *here is a list of existing texts and other sources you might find helpful'* (But you'll still have to find them for yourself and decide how best to use them.)

4 'As in 3, but *here is a* **study guide** *that will help you learn from the suggested materials once you have obtained them'* (You'll still have to find them yourself, but at least we'll help you learn from them.) (See **projects**.)

5 'As in 4, but *we'll provide you with the materials as well as the study guide'* (We'll help you learn from material that was either not intended for learners at all or just not for learners like you.)

6 'As in 5, but *these are materials specially written for materials-based learners not unlike you'* (We'll help you learn from teaching materials even though they don't exactly suit your specific **needs**.)

7 'As in 6, but *these are teaching materials we've written specially for learners like you with all necessary study help built into them.'* (We'll teach; you can learn.)

Needless to say, options towards the top of the list (once familiar to students of the London University external degree scheme) are cheap for the providers and expensive for the learners. Towards the bottom of the list (with the more **user-friendly** approaches common in the Open University and many training contexts) the reverse is true.

Which approach does *your* situation demand? Which approach can your budget (and that of your learners) afford?

Media—*how best to carry the message?*

Many MBL projects go adrift because the wrong media have been chosen. Or because a medium suitable for some of our teaching purposes is press-ganged into use for all of them.

It is too easy to get seduced (or put off) by the razzmatazz of the latest gismo – and it always has been, right through from printed texts to virtual reality. However powerful, exciting and well funded the new medium might be, it may still not be the most appropriate for *this* purpose, for *these* **learners** and in *this* situation. On the other hand, it may be exactly right on all counts.

Here are some criteria to help guide your choice of media.

- Do any of the learning **objectives** dictate certain media?
- Which media will be physically available to the learners and convenient for them to use?
- Are any media especially likely to help motivate learners?
- Is your organization pressing you to use certain media?
- Which media will you be most comfortable with?
- Which media will learners already have the necessary **study skills** to use?
- Which media do you have the necessary skills to use?
- Which media will you be able to afford to use?
- Which will your learners be able to afford to use?

Choosing may not be easy. You may find there are conflicts – eg between what your learners would most benefit from and what you can afford or have the skills to provide. Perhaps the most useful question to ask is: 'What is the simplest and cheapest medium (or combination of media) that will adequately (even if not perfectly) meet our learners' needs?' (See **technology**.)

Try to *avoid* being forced to:

✗ decide on a medium before you've thought through your learners' needs and the objectives/**content** of the teaching

✗ use a medium simply because it's available or urged upon you by someone else

✗ go for a high-tech ('powerful') medium in the belief that it will automatically be more effective than a simpler one

✗ choose a medium that will unduly limit learners' **access** to your programme.

Mentors—*a shoulder to lean on*

The idea of mentoring is still new to many organizations. Yet in others, like Jaguar Cars, Bank of Scotland and many health authorities, it has become so much part of the system that regular training is provided for potential mentors.

The most important function of the mentor is to give the **learner** someone to talk to. He or she might be:

- someone on whom the learners can try out new ideas

- someone who will encourage the learners to reflect on what they are learning and how it relates to their life and work and

- someone who will look out for their interests in the organization.

He or she is the learners' ally and perhaps their **champion**.

Ideally, one should perhaps have someone other than one's **line manager** as mentor. In civil service training, people sometimes call this the 'grandfather/grandmother' role – to distinguish it from the perhaps more parental role that people may ascribe to their line manager. Learners should be able to talk freely with their mentor, knowing that she or he has no direct power to retard or advance their career.

If learners also have a **tutor**, then there may be no need for their mentor to be an expert in the subject they are studying. They may even look outside the workplace for a mentor and enlist a friend or relative in the role.

But the role of mentor is still evolving. Often she or he is an unplanned amalgam of tutor, adviser and friend. Sometimes an organization will argue that the mentoring functions are being carried out by someone who is not called a mentor and who may also be responsible for supervising the learner, reporting on their progress or even carrying out **assessment**. Such additional tasks, however, may weaken their appeal as a mentor and leave the learner still in need of this desirable form of **support**.

Organizations setting up a learning support system may want to consider what the learner needs that cannot be provided by tutors, line managers, trainers and other staff. And, if someone is to be asked to meet such needs as a mentor, how are they to be prepared for and supported in that task – and what **rewards** might be in it for them?

Milieu—*concerning 'what it feels like'*

I once chatted with some trainees in the back room of a retail store where, surrounded by various debris and the noise from some kind of generator, they were doing their best to work through a **package** of training materials by the light of a naked overhead bulb. They told me: 'The boss says Head Office wants us to do this, but our mates reckon we're just trying to escape from the customers. They call us "wozzocks"!'

So what is going on here? The French have given us a word for it – for that often overlooked but very powerful factor in learning – that combination of influences that determines the way we feel about learning (or teaching) in a given situation. You might call it ethos, ambience, climate, culture or atmosphere, but the word 'milieu' is often used in the literature of teaching and seems to incorporate them all.

Some important aspects of the milieu may be physical – like the cleanliness and state of repair of the places in which learners learn or the visual and tactile quality of the **materials** or equipment they are working with. But the most powerful influences are *social* – the attitudes, values and expectations people express to one another and the sometimes different ones they convey by the way they actually behave. Do your learners feel encouraged, well provided for and part of a learning community (even though they may be distant from one another)? Or neglected, abused and on their own? Are they industrious and enthusiastic or lethargic and cynical?

Even in 'conventional' learning, different programmes may create quite different milieux. A college milieu may be quite different from that of a training department; but in either case, one programme may, for example, be felt as cold, formal, impersonal, bureaucratic, uncaring and competitive while another feels, warm, friendly, person centred, caring and collaborative. The milieu may never be explicitly discussed but it will still affect people's **motivation** to learn
– and hence what they learn and how well they learn.

Whether on-site or at a **distance**, there is much you can do to improve the learning milieu. Many of the pages in this book are relevant – eg see: **assessment, attitudes, briefing, course guides, feedback, glue, help lines, line managers, mentors, individualization, newsletters, self-help groups, stress, support, user-friendliness** and **workload**. Since few of us can sustain a milieu on our own, you might also want to consider **staff development** and **institutional support**.

Monitoring—*your hand on the tiller*

MBL programmes can't be left to run themselves. However sharp your **anticipation**, you won't have got everything right in advance. **Developmental testing** may not have shown up all the flaws in your **materials**. Your **support** plans may fail to work out properly for at least some of your **learners**. And if **tutors** and other colleagues are involved in the programme, they too may run into (or become!) problems. You will probably need to make in-course corrections.

The price of success is continuous vigilance. You will need to think about what kinds of information might help you maintain and improve your programme's **effectiveness**. And – especially if you don't see much of your learners (and any colleagues) – you will need to set up a formal system for collecting it and for appropriate **record-keeping**. Such a system may involve regular inspection of routine statistics, as well as questionnaires, **feedback**, interviews, **quality assurance**, and a good deal of listening to what people are telling you (or not telling you). These efforts will also contribute to **evaluation**.

Here are just a few of the aspects you might want to monitor:

Process aspects:
- Enrolments/**Drop-out**
- Numbers using facilities
- How materials are used
- **Workload** of learners
- **Staff development** activities
- How programme colleagues respond to the unexpected
- Problems faced by learners
- Problems faced by tutors/**mentors**/others
- How learners and support staff work together
- Ways people are modifying the programme
- Whether our processes are in line with our **aims**

Product or outcome aspects:
- How learners and others feel about the programme
- What learners have learned – eg new insights and competences
- Effect on learners' job performance
- Whether the programme affects different groups in different ways
- Long-term effects on the organization
- Cost-effectiveness
- Acceptability to outsiders
- Learner complaints
- Newly revealed needs
- Whether outcomes are in line with our aims

Motivations—*what keeps learners going?*

How can we engage and keep our **learners'** interest? That is often more of a problem for MBL than for 'conventional' teaching, especially when learners miss out on the 'social **glue'** that is spread by regular contact with other learners and with teachers. Some learners may feel peeved that they are being asked to do MBL at all. 'Training is for unemployed people,' they may say. Others may be resentful (and show **resistance**) if they are being expected to do any of the training in their own time: 'Why can't we have a proper course?'

Even if your learners are volunteers, it will pay you to know what they might want from their learning. There are four common **attitudes** – or 'orientations' – to learning:

Vocational – to do with the learner's present or hoped-for job

Academic – to do with interest in a subject for its own sake

Personal – to do with developing oneself as a person

Social – to do with emulating and seeking approval from teachers and peers.

And all but the last of these can be pursued either for *'intrinsic'* or *'extrinsic'* purposes. That is, a person may be (intrinsically) interested in what they are learning. Or they may be (extrinsically) interested in what they hope will *result* from the learning – eg a job, promotion, a pay-rise, a degree, the respect of their partner. The fourth orientation seems purely extrinsic; it can operate without any of the others though it may also powerfully supplement any of them.

Learners with intrinsic motivation tend to work better and achieve more than those with purely extrinsic motivation. Learners with several reasons for studying – eg personal or social as well as academic or vocational – are also more likely to do better than those with one only.

So can we – in marketing our programmes, in **entry counselling**, in designing learning **activities** and **projects**, and in providing learner **support** and encouraging **self-help groups** – promote the *intrinsic* benefits that learners might expect to get from their learning? How might what they learn help them in their work, their family or social life, or in their development as persons?

But also, if you are not providing it already, consider whether **accreditation** might be an additional motivator for some – eg those reluctant work-based learners who might just take the task more seriously if offered a marketable qualification.

Needs analysis—*who needs what?*

What is the purpose of the MBL you are providing? To satisfy learners' needs, right? Well, up to a point. But maybe not simply those of the **learners**. Perhaps they have sponsors, professional bodies, **line managers**, organizations – all of whom may also have needs they expect you to take into account. You may also feel that the standards or traditions of your discipline also impose needs, eg what it means to be a 'credible historian' or a 'safe doctor'. These may even be set out for you in the form of 'occupational standards' or 'competences' which your MBL must help learners towards.

There is often a big difference between 'perceived needs' (what learners say they want) and 'prescribed needs' (what other people say they should have). My colleague Tony Kaye recounts how a company's training department once asked him to develop a lengthy MBL course on 'Principles of Chemistry' for process workers who were letting too many errors through. After discussions with the workers and their managers, and observations at the plant, the training 'need' was met instead by attaching new charts to the machinery!

Here are some ways of exploring needs with your learners and those closest to them:

- Interview and run 'focus groups' with potential learners.
- Observe people already doing the job to which the learning relates (including 'master performers').
- Interview their line managers.
- Try doing the job yourself.
- Analyse **job descriptions**.
- Get master performers to tell you about 'critical incidents' in their work, ones that required all their skills.
- Analyse tasks into their separate components.
- Study the recurring errors, faults or lapses of **quality** that appear in people's work.
- Analyse the social interactions involved in a job.
- Ensure that each entrant to your course is offered **entry counselling** to identify how their *individual* needs might differ from those of entrants in general.

Perhaps you are not providing for work-based learners? Maybe your course will be more clearly academic. If so, how can you be sure you are balancing perceived and prescribed needs? What might be the role of **market research?**

Networking—*who can you know?*

Welcome to the 'invisible college'. Possibly you'll already feel loyalty to an organization and maybe also to your profession or discipline. Well now you can feel a further loyalty to all those mostly unknown colleagues around the world – in all kinds of organizations and professions – who are as involved as you are in MBL.

In MBL, as elsewhere, what makes a difference is not just what you know but also *who* you know. So you might start getting to know some of those invisible co-workers around the world. They could be a fruitful and supportive resource for you to draw on – as could you for them. You might be able to swap ideas for courses, sources of useful **existing materials**, samples of your own **materials**, experiences about what works and what doesn't, suggestions for improvements, offers of help, ideas about handling the politics of MBL and, when things are not running too smoothly, moral support and, if you're interested, a job in MBL (or out of it) elsewhere!

Perhaps the place to begin networking is in your own back yard. Are colleagues elsewhere in your organization already engaged in MBL? If so, what might you all gain by making contact? Might you even be able to act as one another's **champions**? I have just run a **workshop** in one organization where several departments are politely pursuing MBL despite equally polite hostility from the organization. The workshop members resolved to keep in touch by e-mail and monthly seminars, thus operating as a mutual support group.

Beyond your own organization, you may be able to meet people at workshops and courses or at conferences and exhibitions relating to MBL. I know that many people who have taken part in my workshops and courses over the years have stayed in touch with one another, even though they come from quite different organizations and even countries.

If you have **Internet** access, you may also want to join (free) some of the international online discussion groups you think might be relevant to your interests. For example:
To join DEOS-L (on distance education) or TRDEV-L (on training and development), send the message 'SUBSCRIBE DEOS-L (or TRDEV-L) Your first name and surname' to 'LISTSERV@PSUVM.PSU,EDU'.

If you can't find a suitable online discussion group, why not start one? You are never entirely alone if you can network!

Newsletters—*what's been happening?*

People working in an MBL system can easily get isolated from one another. They may be working in different places and at different times; and they may not fully appreciate how their work relates to that of other people in the system.

So, course developers may be unaware of what the **support** staff are doing; one supporter (eg a **tutor** or learner's **line manager**) doesn't know what others supporters are doing; **champions** within the organization are not up to date on the project; past and potential clients or sponsors are unaware of the excellent work being done; learners are out of touch with other learners; and the person **managing** the system is too busy to keep everyone else well informed.

Is any of this likely to be true of your own MBL system? If so, you might consider compiling a regular newsletter. This need not be a massive item. In fact, it is more likely to be read if it occupies no more than one A3 sheet or – if you decide to send it by e-mail – the equivalent of four A4 pages. Perhaps it is more important to ensure that it is fairly regular – say once a month (provided there is enough to report).

You will know best what you might most usefully put in your newsletter. Here are some items I might put in mine:

- updates on how the project is progressing

- advice/reassurance about problems that have arisen

- celebration of problems overcome and goals achieved

- requests for **feedback** on ideas for new projects

- reports from support staff sharing their 'good practice'

- letters from colleagues asking for help or ideas

- a 'frequently asked questions' column

- news of **staff development** opportunities

- news of similar projects in other organizations

- brief reviews of relevant publications (eg **case studies**).

A successful newsletter can help foster a learning **milieu**, nurturing the feeling of being 'all in this together', swapping ideas and experience with 'other people like us' and sharing the **ownership** of a worthwhile and effective project. But don't ignore other aspects of **communication**. The best of newsletters is no substitute for getting around and talking with people – and paying attention to what they tell you.

Objectives—*what will they learn to do?*

One of the biggest mind-shifts in my nearly-40 years in education has come with the 1960s' rediscovery of objectives. This helped move the focus of attention from the teacher teaching to the **learner** learning. Instead of asking what the teacher plans to do with the learner, we can ask what the *learner* might be expected to do (or do better) as a result.

So, we are no longer content to hear general aims for a course, eg that learners should 'understand and appreciate the need for a balanced diet'. Instead, we want to know more specifically what learners can expect to be able to do at the end of the course that they were unable (or less able) to do when they started, eg 'List the important components of food; state what each provides for the body; interpret food composition tables; calculate the quantity of components in sample diets; evaluate sample diets against recommended dietary intake; plan a balanced diet for given individuals.'

Such clarity about intentions helps *teachers* and *trainers* to:

- decide the **content** and **structure** of a course
- choose appropriate teaching **media**
- design appropriate learning **activities**
- inform colleagues about their teaching plans
- design appropriate **assessment** and **evaluation**

. . . and helps *learners* to:

- decide whether the course suits their **needs**
- know what it will demand of them
- identify objectives of their own
- allocate their time appropriately
- weigh up their progress and achievement
- review their work on the course.

A credible MBL **course specification** needs to have objectives (and/or the very similar 'learning outcomes' or 'competences') clearly spelled out – for the course as a whole and for individual units and sections within it. A specific statement of what learners will learn to *do* will shift the focus from the content teachers will be teaching to what learners can be expected to *achieve*. As Robert Mager, a US guru of objectives, pointed out some years ago: 'If you don't know where you're going, you're liable to land up someplace else.'

Ownership—*sharing it around*

I remember once taking part in a discussion where I and a couple of Open University colleagues had gone to meet a group from another college. The idea was that we might be collaborating with them in developing a new course. Every time we made a suggestion, the people in the other group cut us off with something like: 'Yes, we've already thought of that' or 'We've been doing that for weeks' or 'That's old hat around here.' To their surprise, we quickly decided they didn't want **collaboration**. We went off to produce our own version of the course, leaving them to produce theirs.

Similarly, I was once involved with an MBL operation where staff had learned to do nothing until they were told exactly what to do. What they did, while competent, was uninspired and the climate was diligent rather than creative. It struck me as ironic that a system supposedly dedicated to developing the autonomy of its **learners** allowed little or none to its staff.

In most working **teams**, people's **motivation** is greatly affected by how much ownership they feel in the project. Do they feel that it is, in some sense, 'their' project? Or do they feel they are mere serfs labouring on someone else's? This may partly depend on the level of **institutional support** they feel they are getting. More specifically, it will depend on the style and approach of whoever is **managing** the project.

How do you feel about the management of projects you've worked on? My most productive experiences have been with teams in which:

- decision-making is done *with* staff rather than *for* them

- staff know that they are expected to put forward their ideas

- ideas will be listened to and will not be ridiculed or penalized and

- their contribution to the plans will be publicly acknowledged.

You may also want people *outside* your immediate team to share in the ownership of the project – other people in your organization, learners, learners' sponsors or **line managers**. This can be achieved through **consultation**. Let them see that the project team values their experience and suggestions – eg get them to comment on plans, circulate their ideas (eg in **newsletters**) and make sure your **materials** contain a printed acknowledgement of their contribution.

Pacing—*keeping up with one's peers*

A few months ago I visited a trainer whose class were all working individually on computer-based **packages**. She said 'I'm a great believer in independent learning, You see, all these people are learning at their own best pace' – and, then, without intentional irony, 'and I decide what that is'!

Pacing has long posed a dilemma for fans of materials-based learning. On the one hand, it does allow a person to learn at their own pace, being neither held up by slower classmates nor holding up faster ones. Indeed it is part of the philosophy of open learning: 'learning at your own time, place and pace'. On the other hand, **learners** left *completely* free to decide when and how long to study – especially if the course is a lengthy one – prove only too likely to drift, lose their momentum and become **drop-outs**. Most learners gain heart from knowing that they are moving through a series of learning experiences and meeting targets at roughly the same rate as their peers and are not being left way behind.

So, if you want to do your best by your learners, there may be a compromise to be struck between the attitude of 'We're all big girls and boys now, so it's not my business to make you learn faster than you wish' and one of 'I know what's best for everyone, so learn exactly when and as long as I tell you.' However much we wish to encourage the autonomy of our learners, they may reasonably expect us to lay down some broad guidelines that will help them stay with the course.

So you may need to **structure** your course in such a way that it limits your learners' freedom to take their own time. Here are just a few of the pacing devices you may want to build in:

- an end-of-course **examination** at a fixed date

- all **assignments, projects** and other coursework to be completed by a certain date near the end of the course

- **deadlines** for handing over of assignments, etc spaced at two- or three-week intervals throughout the course

- weekly **computerized tests** which they must pass

- occasional **face-to-face sessions** which learners must prepare for if they are not to lose face with their peers

- regular check-up calls from their **tutor**.

Whatever constraints you impose, learners should know that you *can* relax them if they run into real problems – eg by extending deadlines and even allowing examination resits.

Packages—*materials with a purpose*

Much MBL depends on specially compiled learning packages. That is, **learners** aren't simply given a reading list and left to forage in understocked **libraries** or let loose on the **Internet**. Instead, they are provided with collections of **material** (books, articles, videos, audio-tapes, computer software, or whatever) that some teacher or trainer has (a) brought together and/or (b) specially developed with those particular learners' needs, and the **objectives** of the course, in mind.

The package of materials will be meant to substitute for at least some direct help from a teacher, and possibly for help from other learners also. Thus, it may need to:

- get the learners interested
- remind them of earlier learning
- tell them what they will be learning next
- explain new ideas to them
- relate these ideas to learners' own experience
- get learners to think and use the new ideas
- help them get **feedback** on how they use them
- encourage them to practise
- make sure they know what they're meant to be doing
- enable them to check their own progress
- help them to do better.

Some organizations, like the Open University and many training groups, develop integrated, custom-built 'open learning' packages. These may contain materials in several **media** (eg text, video, audio, CD-ROM). Each item in such a package will have links to the others and each will probably need to contain elements like those in the list above.

An alternative form of package – common in resource-based learning – is to build the teaching around a collection of **existing materials**. This can save hugely on **production** time.

Perhaps the three most important questions to ask in evaluating your own or someone else's package are:

- Is it **user-friendly** – in level, examples, **readability**, format?
- Does it involve learners in appropriate **activities** ?
- Are learners given adequate **briefing** on how to use it?

Practical work—*how it can be done*

Forget 'Brain Surgery by Correspondence' and 'The Teach Yourself Book of Lion-taming'. But don't give up the idea of MBL merely because your **learners** need practical work and you assume it can't be provided. Even if you rarely meet your learners, even if they are learning at a **distance**, there is usually a way. For instance, you may be able to:

- provide video or audio+print materials that demonstrate procedures and talk the learner through practising them

- have learners work with computer-based simulations

- make use of resources available in the learners' context – eg household or workplace resources, local facilities or events, friends and colleagues

- provide 'practical kits' containing all the materials that learners need to carry out observations, manipulations, experiments, data-collection, surveys, etc

- enable learners to do practical work in occasional **face-to-face sessions**, eg at learning **centres** or summer schools

- arrange with outside organizations to make practical facilities at their premises available to your learners

- set up **projects** in which learners can share resources.

But first, consider these questions:

- What kind of practical work seems needed – eg work with equipment, with materials or with other people?

- Why is it needed – eg to improve learners' ability to handle equipment, carry out procedures, respond to messy reality, work effectively with people?

- Can any of your purposes be met in some other way – eg demonstrations on video, or paper-based **activities**?

- What equipment or facilities are needed and how will they be obtained and funded?

- Will the practical work need **developmental testing**?

- How can learners be given a sufficiently detailed **briefing**?

- Are there problems of safety, security, equal opportunities?

- How will learners get **feedback** on their practical work, eg from self, peers, **tutor**, **mentor**, **line manager**, etc?

- What briefing might such supporters need?

- Will you need to arrange for the **assessment** of practical work, eg to ensure that learners do it?

Prerequisites—*before you begin . . .*

The UK's Open University is an institution devoted to materials-based learning. In fact, despite its early nickname of 'university of the air', the learning has been predominantly print-based. To use the old cliché, our students literally do 'read for a degree'. And yet, 25 years went by before someone suggested we should check what level of reading skills our new entrants bring with them. When we did, we found that nearly one third of them are likely to have difficulty with the kinds of texts they are expected to study in foundation courses.

So, shall we continue to let anyone enrol, on the understanding that they'll become **drop-outs** when they find they can't cope? Or shall we test their reading skills when they first apply and counsel them out before they waste their time and money? (Yes, I know there's the option of improving the **readability** of our materials, and we're working on that as well.)

But here is the basic question: just what does our MBL course or programme require of **learners** *before* they begin? What, if anything, are we expecting by way of prerequisite:

- knowledge of the subject **content**
- skills (including **study skills**) and
- **attitudes** and **images of learning**
- experience (eg in academic, workplace or life situations)
- attainment in previous courses?

We can't afford to be too prescriptive or we won't get enough learners. Nor can we afford to be too *laissez-faire* or we'll get too many drop-outs. (Unless we build a catch-up course alongside our programme – and give the less advanced learners longer to complete it.)

So it is important for a course development **team** to decide what prerequisites they'll be demanding before they begin work. And as the course emerges, we should check whether we've stuck to these intentions. (I've seen courses say 'all you need is the ability to add, subtract, multiply and divide' and then, soon afterwards, plunge the unsuspecting learner into a mind-boggling torrent of algebraic symbolism.)

So, in all course publicity and in **entry counselling,** make clear to learners any prerequisite knowledge, skills, attitudes and experience the course will demand of them. If necessary, devise a diagnostic test that enables them to decide for themselves whether they have what it will take.

Production—*getting your course out*

If your MBL course uses only **existing materials**, there's no great problem. Choose the **materials**, sign your cheque, arrange storage, work out a system for getting items to and from your learners, and you're just about done. (Though you may need to write a **study guide**.) But if you feel compelled to develop your own materials, then you haven't even started.

Here are just some of the questions to which you may need to find answers.

- What budget is available for developing and evaluating the course?

- Over what **time** period must the course be produced?

- Who will be involved in the project and what will be their individual **roles** and responsibilities?

- Do you need to recruit new staff or **consultants**?

- Who will arrange training or **staff development**?

- Will you need **collaboration** with other organizations?

- Who will develop a **course specification**?

- What stages will each set of materials go through – eg first draft, **commenting**, second draft, editing and house-styling, **developmental testing** and **feedback** to author, third and final draft, multiple copying of materials?

- Who will 'sign off' the drafts at each stage and using what criteria?

- How will you **schedule** the various stages?

- How will you produce multiple copies – eg photocopying, offset litho, laser printing, commercial printers?

- Who will manage the project, supervise the work of the team, liaise with other parts of the institution and others?

- How will you store the materials and organize their distribution to learners?

- What will you do about developmental testing to improve the course materials while they are still being developed and about **evaluation** once they are being used by learners?

- What contingency plans can you make (eg jettison parts of the course or draft in extra staff) in case production falls behind schedule?

No doubt *you* will see yet more issues that need thinking about.

Projects—*doing their own thing?*

Do you believe in asking your **learners** questions to which you don't know the answers? Do you want them to draw on resources other than those you have included in the course? Do you want them to relate the course's ideas to their own interests and individual contexts? Do you aim for them to develop as autonomous learners capable of organizing their own development independently of teachers or trainers?

If so, you may want to build a **project** into your course. That is, for some substantial part of the course – say 50 hours or more – you may want learners to pursue an enquiry of their own. This might mean searching databases, interviewing, designing or evaluating, preparing an exhibition, working with people – whatever is relevant to your course **objectives**.

Project work encourages learners in developing higher-level skills than are called upon by most **activities**, and by information-delivery **images of teaching**. It can, for example, exercise the learner's ability to identify problems they can manage, plan an approach, collect data, decide priorities, relate their course knowledge to their own 'real world', evaluate their findings, make something useful of them, communicate their findings, collaborate with other people, and so on.

Most learners rise to the challenge and often find it the most stimulating and productive part of their course. Others will feel uncomfortable about taking such responsibility for their own learning and may need more guidance and influence from their supporters. All learners need careful **briefing** for such work and plentiful **support** – eg in deciding on a topic that is manageable within the time available, in deciding a plan of action and in preparing their analysis or presentation – and in ensuring that they don't get so carried away that they neglect other parts of the course!

Tutors or **mentors** can give this support most easily, perhaps, if the learner has to report progress by certain **deadlines** (maybe in the form of **assignments**). **Help lines** will also probably be more in demand than usual. The **assessment** of a learner's project needs to give at least as much weight to how they defined and set about their task and what they learned from it as to the quality of their final report or presentation.

Course developers may be happy that, on a course where 50 per cent of the learning time consists of a project, nearly 50 per cent less **material** needs developing. But any savings there will most likely need to be spent on providing more time from supporters.

Quality assurance—*showing you care*

MBL systems abound with horror stories. I hear of poorly presented **materials**; materials delivered to **learners** late; learning **centres** shut when they are supposed be open; equipment with long-standing faults; lost **assignments**; inconsistent marking; untraceable learners; demoralized staff; and so on, and on. Worst of all, I hear of systems that have no means of getting early warning of such lapses of quality and correcting them (let alone preventing them).

What might you need to do to enhance the quality of your MBL operation? Can you go beyond the old approach of quality *control* – inspecting poor quality *out* towards one of quality *assurance* – designing good quality *in*?

If your organization or project already has a system for quality assurance:

- Do all staff know the policy on quality and where the most damaging lapses of quality are liable to occur?

- Were staff and learners consulted in developing the policy and their experience and suggestions taken into account?

- Have *standards* of quality – eg for materials and for **support** services – been made clear to all concerned?

- Are these reasonable, measurable and achievable?

- Are they clearly related to **customers'**/clients' satisfaction?

- Have the *procedures* needed for quality been made clear to all concerned?

- Is there a **monitoring** system to check that standards are being met and procedures followed?

- Do its findings lead to corrective action being taken?

- Are people **rewarded** for achieving high quality?

- Are enough efforts devoted to finding out what support staff need to help them maintain quality standards?

- Is adequate support and **staff development** provided?

- Can staff suggest any ways of improving the quality of the quality assurance system?

And if your organization has no system, how might notions like those listed above help you and your colleagues to devise one? What sort of a system can you set up to close any quality loopholes – ideally making things 'right first time' – so that learners, clients and staff get what they are entitled to expect?

Readability—*how plain is your prose?*

Print is still the chief medium for teaching and learning in MBL. Even with many new **technology**-based media like CD-ROM, multimedia and, especially, **computer conferencing** and the **Internet**, learners spend most of their study time *reading*.

But, whether we are presenting our text on paper or on screens, how readable is it? Much of the prose we find in textbooks and training manuals is hard to make sense of. Why? It is not all due to the difficulty of the ideas being expressed. As T.S. Eliot said, there is a difference between 'the expression of obscurity and obscurity of expression'.

Obscurity of expression most often arises because authors have used too many long sentences, too many long words and too many passive verb forms.

Unclear writing is bad news for **learners**. In this television age, fewer and fewer learners have the **study skills** or patience for decoding unclear texts (or for any serious reading). Lack of clarity, especially when coupled with a heavy **workload**, encourages learners to take a surface-level approach to the course **content** and skip as much of it as they think they can get way with. They are more likely to become **drop-outs**.

Happily, we can measure the readability of our writing. Several different tests are available. They tell us if we may need to break up some long sentences and replace long words with shorter (and usually more familiar) ones.

One well-known measure is Robert Gunning's 'Fog Index':

1 Calculate the average number of words per sentence in a passage.

2 Add on the percentage of words with three or more syllables.

3 Multiply by 0.4 (ie multiply by 4 and divide by 10).

If the result – the Fog Index – is more than 12, your text could be too difficult for most of your readers.

If you are writing with a computer, your word-processing package may save you the arithmetic. Microsoft Word 5, for example, will calculate another readability measure – Rudolph Flesch's 'Reading Ease Score' for what you write.

So whose job will it be to *check* (and improve) the readability of **materials** that your learners will be expected to learn from? And don't forget that any **existing materials** you plan to use may not be as readable as those you would write yourself.

Record-keeping—*what are they up to?*

By definition, materials-based **learners** spend less time than others with their teachers. So they are less visible. It is easy to lose sight of them. In addition, they may be much freer to choose their own sequence through a course or to go at their own **pace**. So different members of one cohort of learners may be at very different points in a course at any one time.

Here are just *some* of the many issues you may find it necessary to record about individual learners:

- how they were recruited
- who, if anyone, is sponsoring them
- their prior education, training and experience
- which of your courses they have studied previously
- why they are studying what they are studying now
- any special problems or lack of facilities
- where they have got to in the present course
- what they have produced so far
- attendance at **face-to-face sessions** or **centres**
- results of **assessment** exercises
- strengths and weaknesses observed by **tutors**
- complaints they may have made
- what they do when the course is finished
- subsequent news of them.

Furthermore, many members of the course development **team** or the learner **support** team may also be working at a **distance**. They too may be lost sight of (until too late) unless someone records their comings and goings. Which of their activities might you need to make note of?

Needless to say, keeping the records is not the point of the operation – *using* them is. So who can tell us where each learner is in terms, for example, of courses done so far, **assignments** completed and grades achieved on the present course, strengths and weaknesses, special problems? Can they quickly identify learners in danger of falling behind or dropping out? Can they tell us which tutors have been giving less than acceptable **feedback** or getting falling attendance at face-to-face sessions? Can they describe current trends in enrolment, **drop-out** and what successful learners go on to do next? Such records can play a crucial role in **evaluation**.

Resistance—*why do we have to?*

Not everyone will be as keen on MBL as you are (assuming you are, that is). This can be a problem (challenge) if you are trying to introduce MBL into an organization – or even into a new area of an organization that is already using it in other areas – or even if you are trying merely to introduce new *forms* of MBL. You may meet resistance.

People's **attitudes** to new schemes can be unhelpful for a variety of reasons, eg:

- They haven't been consulted about what is proposed.
- They don't see why the scheme is necessary.
- They believe such schemes have failed in the past.
- They don't trust the people who are proposing the scheme.
- Their cherished values seem threatened, eg 'We'll lose the human dimension' or 'The quality of learning will suffer'.
- They fear not being able to cope with something new or learn new ways.
- They fear loss of status, security, money, time, influence.
- They fear they may be making themselves redundant.

Even within an organization that has already adopted MBL, we can run into such barriers if we try to do it differently. If, for example, the computers and **support** systems are geared up to enrol hundreds of **learners** once a year, we may be told they can't handle a course that would enrol small numbers of learners one-off as soon as they want to start. Again, if our organization insists that plans for programmes must be approved by committees that meet once every three months, how can we take on an innovative project where the sponsor wants a programme up and running in six weeks?

Such attitudes are often the outward expression of more basic causes – the undiscussed **feelings**, the vested interests, the established practices, the ways in which members of staff are motivated, rewarded and managed.

Resistance can only be avoided or overcome through **consultation** and negotiation. We need to help colleagues to identify with the **benefits** of MBL, share in its **ownership** and receive proper **rewards**.

Rewards—*is it worth their while?*

John Wycliffe's reward for his efforts in MBL – improving our access to biblical understanding by translating the scriptures into English – was to have his body dug up and burned, with the ashes being scattered in the nearest river.

Later workers have been more fortunate, though not always as fortunate as they might have deserved. Teachers and trainers, for example, who spend hours of their own time writing materials that will make independent learning possible are often 'rewarded' by being given more classes to teach face to face – while carrying on using their own time to support the independent **learners**. In effect, they have been punished for making their teaching more efficient.

Similarly, **line managers** are often expected to support workplace learners using MBL while still pursuing their previous duties as productively as before. But they may be offered no financial reward, no training or **institutional support** themselves in this new role – and therefore gain no satisfaction other than hanging on to a job that's becoming more and more a source of **stress**.

Here is what one colleague from another university told me, talking of a department that had pioneered MBL within that university:

> 'We depend on the academic staff to write modules for the BSc course. We provide training and support, and as you may remember, produce some good material. Many of our staff enjoy the process, but they have many demands on their time, particularly the pressure to research and publish. Although our modules are published and copyrighted, the University does not recognize them for research assessment or for career advancement – for example, in staff appraisals, for probationary or staff promotion interviews. Staff have been told by University panels at such interviews that their time would be better spent writing research papers rather than distance learning material!'

Many staff are already wary of MBL and may easily develop **resistance**. Whether in education or in training, MBL is unlikely to be successful unless people feel adequately rewarded – whether in money, respect, **staff development** opportunities, relief from other duties, promotion chances or other appropriate institutional support – for the new and additional efforts being expected of them.

So how might rewards need to be managed if *your* MBL system is to be successful?

Roles—*so many things to be done*

It is dangerous to embark on any sizeable MBL project without thinking about all the tasks that may need carrying out and who will do them. Without clear **job descriptions** or **contracts**, colleagues can falsely assume that someone else is carrying out some key task. And they can be resentful if asked to do more than they thought they'd undertaken to do.

The following list mentions many of the possible roles. Some individuals, especially in a small **team**, may have more than one. And, of course, they may not have the titles shown here.

- *Course leader.* Responsible both for getting **materials** of **quality** produced on time within budget and for **monitoring** and maintaining **effectiveness** once the course is running.

- *Course authors.* Subject specialists (usually) who plan the course, choose or write texts and **study guides**, devise audio-visual or computer-based materials and **practical work**, as well as producing **assessment** and **examination** materials.

- *Media specialist.* Technical expert who can help in the development or use of audio-visual material, computer software, multimedia, **conferencing** etc.

- *MBL adviser.* An expert in MBL techniques who may help authors, eg in clarifying their **objectives**, choosing and using **media**, carrying out **evaluation** or **staff development**, rewriting materials where necessary.

- *Librarian.* Information specialist who may help authors track down **existing materials** and other useful sources.

- *Editor.* Helps authors polish their texts, checks for 'house-style' and prepares final drafts for production.

- *Copyright specialist.* Identifies where authors are reproducing source material that needs **copyright** clearance and chases up the necessary permissions.

- *Graphic designer.* Responsible for layout, typestyle, graphics and the overall physical format of the materials.

- *Tutor.* Provides learner **support**, eg by running **face-to-face sessions** or a **help line** and by marking **assignments**.

You may see the need for yet other roles – eg researcher, subject expert, secretary, training **needs analyst**, marketing expert. And deciding on roles is just the start. You then need to decide who is competent to carry them out. Might some best be done by **consultants**? What **briefing** and **staff development** will be needed? What will be involved in **managing** the team?

Scheduling—*what's to be done by when?*

If you are planning the **production** of any substantial body of
materials, and you're not doing it alone, then you'll need to
agree a schedule with your **team**. Everyone must know what he
or she is expected to produce and by when. This is especially
vital if some members need to see or even **comment** on drafts of
another's work before they can get on with their own.

Working out a schedule can reveal potential snags and
bottlenecks – especially when several authors are writing
different amounts of material, at different speeds, and may
complete their drafts in some order different from that in which
learners will need them for **developmental testing**.

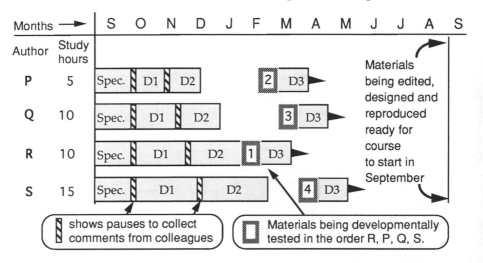

The schedule above, for instance, shows a 40-hour course being
written by four authors, P, Q, R and S, who are responsible for,
respectively, 5, 10, 10 and 15 hours' worth of learning materials.
We see that authors P and Q will, at one point, have a break of
two months or more before they can start on their final drafts
(D3s). This is because learners must test author R's D2 material
before theirs, yet it will not be available for testing until some
time *after* theirs.

But do learners really need to test the D2s in that sequence? (If
not, P's and Q's material could be tested earlier. They could thus
get their D3s completed earlier and thereby spread the load on
editor, designer and **production** facilities.) Or maybe P and Q
could use some of their slack time to help S and R?

What kinds of decisions might a schedule help *you* to make?

Self-help groups—*learner to learner*

Learners on MBL courses may find they don't spend as much time with other learners as they do on 'conventional' courses. This may suit some; but many will feel the loss. Distance learners especially are likely to feel isolated.

What might they be missing? Here are some comments from learners about what they've gained from one another:

- 'There's always someone who's understood a point that's got me foxed and who can explain it better than in the **materials**. And I can sometimes do the same for others.'

- 'Even when I've looked at an issue from every possible angle, someone's always got a different approach.'

- 'Just finding out that I'm not the only one who's having difficulty has been a great consolation to me.'

- 'I like comparing approaches to learning – how do other people cope with the **workload**, how do they tackle the **assignments**, how do they get on applying it at work?'

- 'I've got most out of discussing one another's assignments and the marks and comments we've got – and using that to suss out what the **tutor** is looking for.'

- 'Just the commitment to meeting regularly with the others – a great incentive to getting on with the work.'

- 'We help each other take a broader view of the course – because of our different interests and work-experience.'

- 'Revising together for **exams** – that's when it pays off.'

'Self help groups', where learners help one another, can play an important role in sharing ideas, providing moral **support**, and reducing **stress** and **drop-out**. Getting them set up may not be easy, however, especially with *distance* learners. One approach is to get them together for informal gatherings and circulate contact details for those who want to form groups. Groups may also evolve out of the social after-glow of more formal **face-to-face sessions**. If your learners are studying on site, the self-help groups may arise without your help. Even so – especially if learners rarely need to work in the same place at the same time as one another – it may still help to circulate contact details.

The arrival of e-mail and computer **conferencing** has recently begun transforming the running self help groups. Using the right **technology**, even distance learners can share ideas and support via their computer screens and enjoy all the benefits of collaborative learning.

Staff development—*a priority area?*

MBL projects are often set up in a hurry. There may seem too little time to prepare people in advance. And the powers-that-be may not see much necessity for **briefing** or training. Or they may hope that staff will pick up whatever new skills they need as they go along. In any case, staff may be given no time off from normal duties to prepare for their new **roles**.

All this can spell danger for an MBL project. Newcomers often don't realize how much people might need to learn. Some examples: Designing an MBL course can be quite different from planning a classroom course. Writing MBL **materials** can be quite different from any kinds of writing the teacher has done before. The demands on the MBL **tutor** may be quite different from those faced by classroom teachers. And any move into new **technology** makes **learners** of us all.

So, every MBL project should have a strategy for staff development that will be thought about as soon as the project is mooted and evolve *throughout* its life. Here are some possible components of such a strategy:

- a **needs analysis**, to determine the insights, competences and dispositions that the project will demand of staff
- an **appraisal** of all staff involved (administrators, teachers, librarians, **media** specialists, etc) to identify the learning needs (and **feelings**) of each individual
- **briefing** and **debriefing** sessions and information packs, together with explicit **job descriptions**
- **workshops**, seminars and visits to other MBL users
- staff encouraged to enrol as MBL learners themselves
- **newsletters, conferencing** and other means of sharing colleagues' experience and keeping them updated
- working with an external **consultant**
- internship – assisting a more experienced colleague
- supervision and **mentoring** by experienced colleagues
- keeping a reflective diary or building a 'portfolio'
- **accreditation** (eg by vocational qualifications) for new competences as a manager, tutor or developer of MBL
- an **appraisal** system that reinforces the need for continuous staff development and a **reward** system that – whether through extra money, promotion or enriched opportunities – makes it worth people's while.

Stress—*for learners, tutors and all*

As anyone who's experienced it will tell you, materials-based learning can be quite stressful:

- You may feel isolated.

- People keep setting you difficult tasks.

- You're not sure you know enough about your subject.

- You begin to wonder whether you should have got involved in the first place.

- You've not been given enough time to do a good job.

- But you've got **deadlines** to meet.

- And people will be critical of what you produce.

- Their judgements may affect your future.

- And it may be difficult to find someone who'll give you moral support.

And that's just the *course developers*! Planning and writing MBL materials is *not* just a technical matter. The work involves emotions, **feelings** and anxieties. Developers can suffer all kinds of self-doubt, especially if, as often occurs, they are having to produce fast, in a subject area or a **technology** that is new to them, and without adequate provision of **time**, resources or **staff development**. Other **team** members can be either a threat or source of comfort. Minimizing stress becomes a challenge for whoever is **managing** the team.

Tutors too will share many of the stress factors listed above. But they will have a whole lot more on account of their position at the 'sharp end' – coping with the diversity of **learners** (many of them presenting tricky problems) and feeling a personal responsibility for their learning. Who will enable your tutors to share their concerns, get support and dissipate the stress?

And, of course, the list applies equally to *learners*. Any learning can be stressful if your attainment is going to be judged by someone else's standards. Materials-based learning, so far as there is less opportunity to share concerns with other learners, may be that much more so. Effective MBL programmes recognize this and provide a responsive (and stress-reducing) **support** system.

So who might be suffering what kinds of stress in *your* MBL programme and who might do what to reduce it?

Structure—*what are the critical events?*

The composer Schumann once said about listening to music: 'Only when the form is clear to you will the spirit become clear'. The spirit of their courses, even 'conventional' ones, sometimes remains elusive for many **learners**, as one explained to me:

> 'It's hard to see where all the separate sections fit together really. You keep sort of thinking you have a better idea and then you find something else is going to happen which you didn't expect. . . I found out two days ago that the practical books are going to be handed in for assessment, which I hadn't heard anything about – it would have been nice to know before you started.'

Too often learners find they have embarked on a none-too-magical mystery tour, 'one damn thing after another', with no clear landmarks except for an **examination** lowering distantly on the horizon. This uncertainty can cause **stress**, especially for material-based learners who are less able to get enlightenment from **tutors** and other learners.

Much of the success of your MBL programme may depend on how well you inform learners about the key events that lie ahead. You may describe these in a **course guide** and, where possible, discuss them at an induction meeting. Where there is room for **individualization**, you may be able to negotiate some of the structure with learners, eg in **projects**.

Your structure of events will reflect your **images of teaching**. Like a musical concert or a theatrical play, your course will have a beginning, a middle and an end. It will take its participants through a series of experiences, varying in tone and tempo, each leading up to critical moments of conflict or resolution. Perhaps there will even be one or more intervals.

- What are the main blocks or modules within the course and how long are learners expected to spend on each?

- What marks the beginning and end of the main phases?

- What are the critical events?

- Where are the periods of peak effort?

- Are there any breaks or catch-up periods?

- If there are **face-to-face-sessions** or other requirements to be in a certain place at a given time, where do these occur?

- If there are to be **assignments**, what are the **deadlines**?

- If there is to be an examination, when will it be?

Study guides—*enabling the learning*

Education and training is not a matter of delivering information. The most expensively produced **materials** in the world, or the most glittering presentations, will be of no avail unless the **learner** knows what to do with them. If you are producing custom-built Open University-style **packages**, you will probably weave all necessary guidance into the presentation of the information they are studying.

But what if you plan to base your teaching on **existing materials**? You may, for instance, have gathered sets of books, articles, videos and computer software which may not have been produced for learners like yours (and perhaps not for any learners). Or you may be expecting your learners, perhaps as part of a **project**, to gather their own materials, eg from **libraries** or the **Internet**.

For these purposes, you may need to produce a 'wrap-around' *study guide* providing essential MBL features (and **user-friendliness**) that are missing from the existing materials. For example:

- guidance on how to use (or find) the materials
- the learning **objectives** that users might hope to attain
- introductions/overviews for each of the items
- advice as to sections that should be (or can be) omitted
- summaries, indexes and glossaries of terms
- clearer explanations of any difficult concepts or issues
- contrasting viewpoints or locally relevant examples
- **activities** and self-tests plus **feedback**
- instructions for **practical work** or projects
- suggestions about working with other people
- **assignments** for discussion with **tutor**, colleagues, etc.

The study guide approach can be a useful, **gradual** way into MBL. It enables a department, or even the individual teacher or trainer, to find out how learners react to MBL without needing massive up-front investment of **time** and money.

Yet it is not always as easy (or as quick) as it looks. Suitable materials may be hard to find (or afford) and how long will they remain available? We also need to analyse them with sharp **anticipation** if we are to develop study guides that really do make up for (rather than add to) their MBL deficits.

Study skills—*learning how to learn?*

How proficient are your **learners** as learners? How skilled are they at organizing themselves for study, managing their time, reading for learning, making and using notes, relating to the distinctive ways of arguing and presenting ideas within your discipline, writing essays or reports, carrying out **practical work**, collaborating with other people and using **media** and new **technology**?

In particular, you may want to know what experience your learners have of *materials-based* learning. Are they prepared for the demands it is likely to make on their self-discipline (and maybe on their families)? And do they have the skills to learn from the particular media you plan to use?

For example, if your programme demands they work with printed materials, how competent are they at learning from text? Recent research into the reading skills of Open University entrants suggested that nearly one-third of them would have difficulty with the prose they encounter in foundation courses. You might find it useful to know what newspapers your learners read and what kind of reading they do as part of their jobs or social life. If they read nothing more taxing than the *Daily Tabloid*, it may be unwise to offer too much material written at *Guardian* or *Times* level.

If you are using newer media, like **conferencing** and the **Internet**, learners may need to learn new ways of using old skills. How else will they be able to manage the huge amounts of information they are likely to be bombarded with while at the same time retaining a properly critical approach?

Familiarity with materials-based learning is likely to increase over the next few years – not least because young people will be working with it before they leave school. But, with so many *different* approaches to MBL, can you be sure that your learners will be familiar with your approach? If not, you may need to help them learn about learning as well as about whatever else you are teaching. Otherwise, expect **drop-outs**.

So what might they need to learn about learning? Can they be helped with this up-front, before they get into their subject? Or (more likely) must the teaching of study skills be integrated with the teaching of that subject? How might learners build on skills and approaches they have used in previous courses or in their everyday, informal learning at home or at work? Who will be responsible for assessing individuals' study skills and helping them develop?

Support—*what kind do learners need?*

High-quality learning **materials** – **study guides**, well-chosen resources and **user-friendly** self-teaching **packages** – are clearly essential to materials-based learning. But they are not sufficient. Unless **learners** are properly supported, the best of materials may fail to help them achieve the desired results. Conversely, through **individualization**, a responsive support system can sometimes help them overcome the weaknesses of learning materials that are not of the highest standard.

Most learners will need someone who can respond to them as *individuals* – someone who can respond to each learner's personal needs and concerns. For example, by:

- discussing their learning **needs** and helping them select appropriate courses
- adapting learning materials to suit their needs.
- offering them general guidance about **study skills** and approaches and help with specific learning difficulties
- marking and commenting on their responses to **activities, projects, assignments**, etc
- encouraging them, **assessing** their progress at intervals and giving them helpful **feedback**
- keeping **records** of their progress
- being available in a crisis on a telephone or fax **help line**, through computer **conferencing** or **face-to-face**
- running remedial 'surgeries' and group sessions
- helping learners widen or deepen their understanding
- helping them apply what they are learning to their jobs
- helping them get support from other people, eg from staff at their workplace or through **self-help groups**
- assessing their understanding and competence at the end of a course and advising them on what to do next.

Will you be providing all such support yourself? Or will your learners need support from other people as well – eg from advisers or counsellors, **tutors, mentors**, their **line managers**, technicians or demonstrators, **library** staff, learning **centre** receptionists, their peers in self-help groups, friends, family, work-mates and others?

If so, what kind of **institutional support** might those *supporters* need? And how will it be provided?

Tutors—*and how they support learning*

Tutors are the most crucial form of learner **support**. Without tutorial support, the best **materials** in the world may prove disappointing. On the other hand, quite basic materials can be effective if **learners** are supported by sensitive and diligent tutors. Tutors take up where the materials leave off. In some MBL systems they will have helped develop the materials themselves. In others they will have been appointed separately from the course developers.

Tutoring is a role for someone expert in the subject that learners are learning about. But their role is not to reteach the **content** of the materials. Rather, it is to help learners make their own sense of what they are learning – and perhaps to critique the materials in terms of their own values and experience. So the tutor also needs to be knowledgeable about learners and about the kinds of difficulty they may have and the kinds of support they might find helpful.

Some tutors will run **face-to-face sessions** – usually in groups – probably with an emphasis on problems, **practical work** or helping learners collaborate in a learning task and benefit from one another's insights and experience.

Much important tutoring is done at a **distance** via **help lines**, **conferencing** or, in some MBL systems (like the UK Open University) via **correspondence teaching**. In the Open University, the tutor's most influential and demanding task is to assess the regular **assignments** that learners send them – and write constructive **feedback** that will help a learner overcome any weaknesses and build on his or her strengths.

Teachers and trainers who are new to tutoring materials-based learners may need careful **briefing** from the course developers and continuing **staff development**. Some may find they need to make a major shift in attitudes, eg:

- from deciding what must be learned to helping the learner decide
- from conveying information to helping the learner learn
- from acting as the critical and impersonal expert to building relationships
- from using **assessment** to decide a grade to assessing in order to help the learner learn (eg by written comments)
- from face-to-face teaching to teaching at a distance
- from putting on a performance to nurturing individuals.

User-friendliness—*but how much?*

When we open up **access** to a course or programme we can tempt in **learners** who might not otherwise have taken part. Some may be new to learning. So will our teaching seem accessible enough to all of these new learners? Will they all be able to cope with what we are offering? For example:

- Will they have appropriate **images of learning, motivations, study skills, prerequisite** knowledge of the subject and helpful **attitudes** towards it?

- Will the **readability** of our **materials** be at a level they can handle?

- Will they have sufficient experience with the **media** we are using (especially if new **technology** is involved)?

- Will they be able to handle the social situation, eg they may be working at a **distance** or not getting much regular **feedback** from **tutors** or other learners?

If questions like these raise doubts in our minds, we may have to give our materials-based learners more help than we've given to 'traditional' learners in the past. We may need to make our programme or course more user-friendly.

We may, for example, need to provide:

- preparatory courses or **packages**
- more **readability** in our texts and more explicit teaching
- different **assignments** with more detailed feedback
- different course topics and **activities**
- more individual **support**
- more **face-to-face sessions** and contact with other learners
- a modified **assessment** system
- more time in which to complete the course.

All this may demand not that you simply revamp your existing course but that you totally *rethink* it.

Of course, *all* learners – not just the less capable ones – will appreciate a user-friendly course. But, beyond a certain point, what seems user-friendly to the latter may seem tedious or patronizing to the former. Unless you can deal differently with different learners within your course, you need to strike a sensitive *balance*. Not user-friendly enough and you lose the less capable learners; too much so and you lose not only the more capable but also, perhaps, some of your **credibility**.

Workload—*don't overdo it*

If you provide more **materials** or demand more work than your **learners** can cope with in the time available to them, you will probably create undue hassle and cost for yourself. And your learners will groan, take short cuts and possibly become **dropouts**. To avoid over-loading them, bear in mind the following rough-and-ready estimates of how long students may take when they are reading text material for study purposes:

Easy text (eg narrative style)   say 100 words per minute.
Difficult text (eg complex argument)   say 40 words per minute.

Hence, one hour of plain reading (no activities) =

'Easy' text	*'Difficult'* text
60 x 100 = 6000 words	60 x 40 = 2400 words
Say 300 words per page	Say 300 words per page
= *20 pages per hour*	= *8 pages per hour*
In 10 hours = 200 pages	In 10 hours = 80 pages
In 50 hours = 1000 pages	In 50 hours = 400 pages
. . . and so on.	. . . and so on.

But some of your learners' time – let's say one third – may be spent not on reading but on doing **activities**, using other **media**, writing **assignments** or **projects**.

If so, in 50 hours of *easy* reading plus activities, they'd have time to read only 2/3 x 1000 = 666 pages	If so, in 50 hours of *difficult* reading plus activities, they'd have time to read only 2/3 x 400 = 266 pages.

If an even bigger proportion of time is spent on activities, etc, then learners will clearly have time to read even fewer pages.

So to avoid overloading your learners, take these steps:

1 Estimate how many words they are being expected to read.

2 Judge what proportion are easy, difficult or moderate.

3 Calculate the number of minutes/hours of plain reading.

4 Estimate and add on the time needed for each activity.

5 Add on the time needed for other media, assignments, etc.

6 Compare the total time you seem to be demanding with the amount that learners can reasonably be expected to spend on your material.

7 Prune the wordage, if necessary, to fit the time available.

8 Check workload via **developmental testing** and **evaluation**.

Workshops—*what makes them work?*

There are many approaches to **staff development**. But I have found workshops to be an excellent way both of kick-starting the process and of helping experienced colleagues with their professional updating.

So what makes a workshop? I believe workshops differ from **lectures**, seminars or presentations in the following ways:

- Their purpose is to improve not merely the participants' knowledge but also their vocational competence and/or confidence. Participants should emerge more capable (and feeling it) about doing some aspect of their jobs.

- They are based on carrying out **activities** (the 'work') rather than listening to a presenter talk about his or her experience and opinions.

- **Feedback** on these activities comes from the workshop leader and also (sometimes chiefly) from fellow **learners**.

- Workshops focus on the experience (either recalled or here-and-now) of the participants rather than on the knowledge of the workshop leader.

- They are not a vehicle for delivering of information (as if an **activity**-deficient distance learning **package** were being presented face to face) but for the thinking through of ideas or practising of skills and for the getting of individualized feedback from one another.

- Participants will be doing much more talking than the leader – perhaps two or three times as much.

- Participants can expect to learn as much, or more, from one another than they will from the mouth of the workshop leader.

- The workshop leader will often learn as much from the participants as they do from the leader.

- The leader (to use a well-worn but still worthwhile cliché) does not so much teach as arrange for learning to take place; he or she is a facilitator, not a fount of all wisdom. Not the 'sage on the stage' but the 'guide on the side'.

- In a workshop, it is the priorities of the participants that are paramount (not those of the workshop leader).

If you want help with running workshops, consult Lewis, 1995 or Lewis and Freeman, 1994, or consider working with a **consultant**. (Might there be a place for the workshop approach in **face-to-face sessions** with your learners also?)

Further reading

The 'literature' on materials-based learning is already immense. The following are just a few of the books I have benefited from in recent years, followed by a list of journals in which you are likely to find yet more useful material and by a few Internet sources that may be of interest.

Books

Bleay, J et al (1994) *Tutoring with the Open Business School*, The Open University, Milton Keynes (A mixed-media open learning package for part-time tutors of Open Business School students but which the tutors of any materials-based learners might find helpful.)

Brown, S & Smith, B (eds) (1996) *Resource-based Learning*, Kogan Page, London (A good book to start with if you're thinking of MBL for on-campus learners.)

Calder, J (1993) *Programme Evaluation and Quality*, Kogan Page, London (A comprehensive guide to evaluating materials-based learning programmes.)

Calder, J et al (1995) *Learning Effectiveness of Open and Flexible Learning in Vocational Education*, Research Series No. 58, Department for Education and Employment, Sheffield (A thorough study comparing MBL with 'conventional' approaches in four further education colleges and in Rank Xerox, Inland Revenue, the Post Office and Safeway.) (See also McCollum & Calder, 1995.)

Collis, B (1996) *Tele-Learning: Digital World*, International Thomson Computer Press, London (Thorough and up-to-date guidance, based on critical investigation, about what the World Wide Web might have to offer to MBL.)

Crabb, G (1990) *Copyright Clearance: a practical guide* (3rd edn), National Council for Educational Technology, London (Never use anyone else's material, from print or any other media, without consulting this guide or McCracken & Gilbart, 1995.)

Davies, WJK (1989) *Open and Flexible Learning Centres*, National Council for Educational Technology, London (A review of the issues involved in setting up and running such centres: funding, staffing, equipment and materials, management and administration.)

Dean, C & Whitlock, Q (1988) *A Handbook of Computer-based Training*, Kogan Page, London (Still a useful starting point for newcomers.)

Department for Education & Employment (annual) *Open Learning Directory*, Pergamon, Oxford (Details of thousands of vocational MBL packages, one of which might just save you from developing your own.)

Ellington, H & Race, P (1993) *Producing Teaching Materials* (2nd edn), Kogan Page, London (A useful basic principles book for teachers and trainers who are new to producing teaching materials.)

Evans, T (1994) *Understanding Learners in Open and Distance Education*, Kogan Page, London (Insights into the wide range of backgrounds, personalities, motivations, abilities and styles to be found among materials-based learners.)

Evans, T & Nation, D (eds) (1993) *Reforming Open and Distance Learning: Critical Reflections from Practice*, Kogan Page, London (Provides many insights into the wider social implications of MBL and where it might be leading us.)

Flesch, R (1949) *The Art of Readable Writing*, Harper & Row, New York (A classic; no-one who wants to write with greater clarity and impact should be without it.)

Fletcher, S (1992) *Competence-based Assessment Techniques*, Kogan Page, London (A practical and readable guide to assessing competence in professional and vocational training.)

Flexitrain (1990) *Being an Open Learning Mentor*, Flexitrain Ltd, Abergavenny (An open learning pack comprising two workbooks and an audiotape, commissioned by the Employment Department.)

Freeman, R & Lewis, R (1995) *Writing Open Learning Materials*, Framework Press, Lancaster (A guide to running staff development workshops for course writers – with photocopiable handouts.)

Gibbs, G *et al* (1994) *Course Design for Resource Based Learning*, The Oxford Centre for Staff Development, Oxford Brookes University, Oxford (A series of booklets showing how MBL has been and can be applied on campus, each booklet featuring a different subject area.)

Gibbs, G *et al* (1994) *Institutional Support for Resource Based Learning*, The Oxford Centre for Staff Development, Oxford Brookes University, Oxford (A companion to the booklets mentioned above, this one focusing on what the institution must do if it wants to foster MBL.)

Gunning, R (1968) *The Technique of Clear Writing*, McGraw-Hill, New York (Like Flesch, an inspiration and true guide. Perhaps you've used his Fog Index?)

Habershaw, S *et al* (1984) *53 Interesting Things to Do in Your Seminars and Tutorials*, Technical and Educational Services, Bristol (If your MBL programme has face-to-face sessions, this book could be very helpful.)

Hamilton, D *et al* (eds) (1977) *Beyond the Numbers Game: A Reader in Educational Evaluation*, Macmillan, London (The classic but highly readable introduction to the theory and politics of evaluation.)

Hartley, J (1993) *Designing Instructional Text*, Kogan Page, London (Practical research-based book about how to write clearly and lay out pages effectively.)

Hawkridge, D *et al* (1988) *Computers in Company Training*, Croom Helm, Beckenham (A critical study of the use of computers in company training; the technology has moved on but the authors' approach and comments are just as relevant today.)

Henry, J (1993) *Teaching Through Projects*, Kogan Page, London (The essential guide to helping learners work on personal projects in MBL courses.)

Hodgson, B (1993) *Key Terms and Issues in Open and Distance Learning*, Kogan Page, London (Cuts through the jargon and confusion of terms and concepts.)

Honey, P & Mumford, A (1986) *The Manual of Learning Styles*, available direct from Dr Peter Honey, 10 Linden Avenue, Maidenhead, Berks SL6 6HB (A practical guide to one useful way of responding to learners' differing needs.)

Jones, A, Kirkup, G & Kirkwood, A (1992) *Personal Computers for Distance Education*, Paul Chapman, London (Case study of the introduction of personal computers into distance courses run by the UK Open University.)

Kember, D (1991) *Writing Study Guides*, Technical and Educational Services, Bristol (A guide to wrapping study guides around existing material – which is itself wrapped around Rowntree, 1990)

Laurillard, D (1993) *Rethinking University Teaching: A Framework for the Effective Use of Educational Technology*, Routledge, London (The main title is unduly restrictive; this book can help us rethink any kind of teaching or training, especially if we are using new technology.)

Lewis, R (1995) *Tutoring in Open Learning*, Framework Press, Lancaster (A guide to running staff development workshops for those who will tutor materials-based learners – with photocopiable handouts.)

Lewis, R & Freeman, J (1994) *Open Learning in Further and Higher Education*, Framework Press, Lancaster (A guide to running staff development workshops for colleagues new to materials-based learning – with photocopiable handouts.)

Lewis, R & Meed, J (1985) *How to Manage the Production Process*, Council for Educational Technology, London (Still helpful on the essentials despite developments in media and production technology since it first appeared.)

Lockwood, F (1992) *Activities in Self-instructional Texts*, Kogan Page, London (All about the role of activities, exercises and questions in self-teaching materials – why have them, how to write them and how to make it more likely that learners will take them seriously.)

Lockwood, F (1994) (ed.) *Materials Production in Open and Distance Learning*, Paul Chapman, London (A useful collection of briefing papers by experienced practitioners on many aspects of planning and presenting courses as well as producing them.)

Lockwood, F (1995) (ed.) *Open and Distance Learning Today*, Paul Chapman, London (Another collection of updating articles from the experts on research and development in many key areas of MBL.)

McCollum, A & Calder, J (1995) *Learning Effectiveness of Open and Flexible Learning in Vocational Education: A Literature Review and Annotated Bibliography*, Research Series No 57, Department for Education & Employment, Sheffield (A companion to Calder *et al* (1995) and a source of more 'further reading'.)

McConnell, D (1994) *Implementing Computer Supported Cooperative Learning*, Kogan Page, London (A book showing how collaborative learning through computer conferencing can enhance MBL.)

McCracken, R & Gilbart, M (1995) *Buying and Clearing Rights: Print, Broadcast and Multimedia*, Blueprint, London (Never use anyone else's material, from print or other media, without consulting this guide or Crabb, 1990.)

Mager, R (1990) *Preparing Instructional Objectives* (2nd edn), Kogan Page, London (The book that got many of us thinking for the first time about what we want our learners to get out of the teaching rather than what we might put into it.)

Mason, R (1994) *Using Communications Media in Open and Flexible Learning*, Kogan Page, London (A useful introduction to the various uses of conferencing in education and training.)

Mason, R & Kaye, A (eds) (1989) *Mindweave: Communication, Computers and Distance Education*, Pergamon, Oxford (A valuable collection of articles about the use of computer conferencing in education and training.)

Morgan, A (1993) *Improving Your Students' Learning*, Kogan Page, London (A book that helps us see things from the learners' viewpoints and so improve what we offer them.)

Morris, M & Twitchen, R (1990) *Evaluating Flexible Learning: A Users' Guide*, National Foundation for Educational Research, Slough (A practical book with helpful guidance on 'performance indicators'.)

Nathenson, M & Henderson, E (1980) *Using Student Feedback to Improve Learning Materials*, Croom Helm, London (Still the classic handbook for anyone wanting to carry out developmental testing.)

NEC (1989) *Implementing Open Learning in Colleges,* National Extension College, Cambridge (A multi-media pack sponsored by the Training Agency.)

OPTIS (1989) *Implementing Open Learning in Organisations,* OPTIS, Oxford (A mixed-media pack sponsored by the Training Agency.)

Paul, R (1990) *Open Learning and Open Management,* Kogan Page, London (A lively book about managing open learning and helping staff move from conventional teaching towards flexible learning.)

Postlethwaite, SN, Novak, J & Murray, H (1978) *The Audio-tutorial Approach to Learning,* Burgess, Minneapolis (A readable and practical text that helped foster on-campus independent learning in the US.)

Race, P (1992) *53 Interesting Ways to Write Open Learning Materials,* Technical and Educational Services, Bristol (Practical and down-to-earth guidance from an experienced author.)

Race, P (1994) *The Open Learning Handbook,* Kogan Page, London (2nd edn) (User-friendly guide to all aspects of materials-based learning.)

Rowntree, D (1985) *Developing Courses for Students,* Paul Chapman, London (An overview of the main issues in course design – content, structure, methods and media, assessment and evaluation.)

Rowntree, D (1987) *Assessing Students: How Shall We Know Them?,* Kogan Page, London (This book explores the underlying problems of optimizing truth, justice and practicability in assessment.)

Rowntree, D (1990) *Teaching Through Self-instruction,* Kogan Page, London (A useful reference text covering all aspects of developing course materials – with many extracts from published packages.)

Rowntree, D (1992) *Exploring Open and Distance Learning,* Kogan Page, London (A comprehensive and critical overview of the field – not so much a 'how to do it' book as a 'what's worth doing' book.)

Rowntree, D (1993) *Teach Yourself with Open Learning,* Kogan Page, London (A book for learners introducing them to MBL in general, which providers need to follow up with an introduction to their course in particular.)

Rowntree, D (1994) *Preparing Materials for Open, Distance and Flexible Learning,* Kogan Page, London (A task-by-task guide to producing learning materials.)

Rowntree, D (1994) *Teaching with Audio in Open and Distance Learning,* Kogan Page, London (How to produce materials in this simple but very effective, and rather neglected, medium.)

Schmeck, R (ed) (1988) *Learning Strategies and Learning Styles,* Plenum Press, New York (A valuable collection of articles about the different ways that learners learn and why.)

Tait, A (ed) (1992) *Key Issues in Open Learning: An Anthology from the Journal* Open Learning *1986–1992,* Longman, Harlow (A collection of articles touching on practically every aspect of MBL.)

Temple, H (1991) *Open Learning in Industry,* Longman, Harlow (A study of materials-based learning in industry with many illuminating examples.)

Thorpe, M (1993) *Evaluating Open and Distance Learning,* Longman, Harlow (Plenty of detail on planning, carrying out and implementing the findings of evaluation, with many interesting thoughts on the potential contribution of evaluation to managing an MBL system.)

Thorpe, M & Grugeon, D (eds) (1994) *Open Learning in the Mainstream*, Longman, Harlow (A well-chosen collection of articles touching on most aspects of MBL.)

Wade, W *et al* (eds) (1993) *Flexibility in Course Provision in Higher Education*, Flexible Learning Initiative, Loughborough University of Technology, Leics (A valuable collection of case studies of MBL approaches in on-campus HE.)

Walkin, L (1991) *The Assessment of Performance and Competence*, Stanley Thornes, Cheltenham (A useful guide to assessing learners' practical abilities, especially in a training context.)

Some journals that carry articles about MBL

- *Active Learning* (journal of the Computers in Teaching Initiative, published by CTISS Publications, University of Oxford)
- *American Journal of Distance Education* (Pennsylvania)
- *British Journal of Educational Technology*
- *Educational Media International* (published by Kogan Page)
- *Distance Education* (Australia)
- *ICDE Bulletin* (International Council for Distance Education, Norway)
- *Innovations in Education and Training International* (published by Kogan Page)
- *Journal of Distance Education* (Canada)
- *OLS News* (from National Council for Educational Technology)
- *Open Learning* (published by Longman, Harlow)
- *Open Learning Today* (newsletter of British Association for Open Learning)

Some useful Internet sources (as at January 1997)

- DeLiberations – an electronic journal about university teaching with a discussion forum on resource-based learning at: **http://www.lgu.ac.uk/deliberations/**
- Journal of Interactive Media in Education – a forum in which to discuss and try out interactive learning media at: **http://www-jime.open.ac.uk/jime/**
- The International Centre for Distance Learning (based at the UK Open University) – a database containing over 30,000 detailed entries describing courses and programmes taught at a distance by more than 850 institutions around the world plus over 8,000 entries describing relevant books, journal articles, etc.: **http://www-icdl.open.ac.uk/**
- KMI – for demonstrations and discussions of new technology in MBL, visit the Open University's Knowledge Media Institute at: **http://kmi.open.ac.uk/**
- Assessment online – a Birmingham University (UK) site demonstrating (with multiple-choice questions for medical students) how assessment might be delivered via the Web at: **http://medweb.bham.ac.uk/http/caa/caa.html**
- Interactive patient examination – a Marshall University (US) site enabling you to work on simulated patients at: **http://medicus.marshall.edu/medicus.htm**
- Databases – with resources of value to MBL specialists and links to institutions offering forms of MBL around the world:
  http://www.education-world.com/db/dist.shtml (Education World)
  http://www2.uncg.edu/cex/dli/dlilinks.html (University of North Carolina)
  http://141.163.121.36/teachinglearning/sedresources/sedresources.html

http://www.oltc.edu.au/infopack/infointr.htm (Open Learning Technology Corporation)
http://www.caso.com/iu.html (The Internet University)

- Web-based courses – assorted sites where you can 'observe' teaching:
  http://www.cryst.bbk.ac.uk/PPS/index.html (Protein structure)
  http://www.curtin.edu.au/learn/unit/ (Anatomy, etc)
  http://www.dist-ed.nhc.edu/facmats/mat220/m220htm/SYLLABUS.HTM (Statistics)
  http://ccat.sas.upenn.edu/teachdemo (Classics)
  http://www.st-andrews.ac.uk/~www_sbms/homesbms.html (Medical)
  http://www.sce.ojgse.edu/iq/03phl01.html (Philosophy)
  http://ollc.mta.ca/disted.html (Antibody molecules experiment)
  http://wwwcream.une.edu.au/materialsIndex.html (Computers in education)
  http://www.geom.umn.edu/~strauss/symmetry.unit/ (Geometry)
  http://www.utexas.edu/world/lecture/ (Many subjects)
  http://mc.cqu.edu.au/subjects/85321/ (UNIX systems administration)

- Spectrum Virtual University – sign up for a (free) online course (or offer to teach one yourself) at: http://horizons.org/

- Demonstration Web campus – showing what might be needed in a Web-based teaching system at: www.ivu.com/college/about/default.html

- Universities and Colleges Staff Development Agency (UK):
  http://www.niss.ac.uk/education/ucosda.html

- Training and Development Resource Center (US-based) but plenty of interest to educators also at: http://www.tcm.com/trdev/

- MAILBASE – a listserver at the University of Newcastle that hosts discussion lists on many academic subjects, as well as MBL-related lists like flexible-learning, cm-collab-learning and distance-learn-research. For details of other Mailbase lists, consult Mailbase's Web page at: http://www.mailbase.ac.uk/ or send the e-mail message 'Send lists full' to 'mailbase@mailbase.ac.uk'.

- TILE.NET – a USA-based listserver running academic discussions like Mailbase but with a world-wide clientele. For details, consult their Web page at:
  http.//tile.net/lists

To join (free) one of the MAILBASE or TILE.NET discussion lists (or any of those mentioned below) send the message 'Subscribe list name Your first name and surname' to the server (the host computer), eg I might send the message 'Subscribe flexible-learning Derek Rowntree' to (in this case) 'mailbase@mailbase.ac.uk'.

List name	Subject	Server
Resodlaa	Distance education (Australia-based)	listserver@usq.edu.au
Deos-L	Distance education (USA-based)	listserv@psuvm.psu.edu
Trdev-L	Training and development (USA)	listserv@psuvm.psu.edu
Learning-Org	Systems thinking	majordomo@world.std.com
Tecadv-L	Advising learners via technology (USA)	listserv@uafsysb.uark.edu
Staff-development	Staff development in higher education	mailbase@mailbase.ac.uk